Cats' A. B. C.

Beverley Nichols, with helper, at his desk at Merry Hall. Courtesy of the Bryan Connon Collection.

BEVERLEY NICHOLS'

Cats'
A. B. C.

With a foreword by
Juliet Clutton-Brock

Timber Press
Portland • London

Photograph of Beverley Nichols is the property of Bryan Connon, reproduced by permission

Drawings by Derrick Sayer

New paperback edition published in 2009 by Timber Press, Inc.

The Haseltine Building   2 The Quadrant
133 s.w. Second Avenue, Suite 450   135 Salusbury Road
Portland, Oregon 97204   London NW6 6RJ
www.timberpress.com   www.timberpress.co.uk

ISBN-13: 978-0-88192-993-5

Printed in China through Colorcraft Ltd., Hong Kong

The Library of Congress has cataloged the hardcover edition as follows:

Nichols, Beverley, 1898 1983
    Beverley Nichols' Cats' A. B. C. / Beverley Nichols ; with a foreword by
        Juliet Clutton-Brock.
        p. cm.
    Originally published: Cats' A. B. C. : Jonathan Cape [1960].
    ISBN 0-88192-581-0
    1. Cats. I. Title: Cats' A. B. C. II. Nichols, Beverley, 1898 1983. Cat's A. B. C.
        III. Title.
    SF447 .N5 2003
    636.8—dc21
                                                              2002033356

Contents

Foreword

When *Beverley Nichols' Cats' A. B. C.* was first published in 1960, the study of animal behaviour was in its infancy and the works of the great naturalist Konrad Lorenz were only just beginning to throw 'New Light on Animal Ways', as one of his first books, *King Solomon's Ring*, was subtitled. Equally, David Attenborough was only just beginning to make his wonderful television films of wildlife. But, although Beverley Nichols' appealing style of writing belongs to this earlier age, he captures the character and behaviour of his beloved cats in a manner that could not be bettered by any animal behaviourist of today.

Following the descriptions of the cat by Rudyard Kipling and Konrad Lorenz as the animal that walks by itself, it has become traditional to think of our cats as solitary animals with their own agenda, but Nichols showed in his utterly delightful books, with their wonderful illustrations, how far this is from the whole truth. Wild cats are by nature predators of small prey such as mice, and for this reason cats are not highly social animals, as are wolves (progenitors of our dogs), which hunt large animals in packs. However, like all carnivores, the behavioural patterns of cats are versatile and flexible, which makes them able to adapt to any environment, so they can survive as feral animals in the Antarctic, or live their whole lives indoors in a luxury flat. Even so, cats can still suffer from boredom and loneliness if not understood and cherished in the way that was clearly the good fortune of 'Four', 'Five' and Oscar, who lived with Beverley Nichols in a house and garden that was perfectly in tune with their needs.

JULIET CLUTTON-BROCK, B.SC., PH.D, D.SC., F.Z.S., F.S.A.
In Cat World, *Desmond Morris described Dr Clutton-Brock as*
'the world's greatest authority on the history of domestic animals'

THE CATS' A.B.C.

BEVERLEY NICHOLS

has written the following books on cats, and
gardens in which cats figure prominently

Down the Garden Path, 1932
A Thatched Roof, 1933
A Village in a Valley, 1934
Green Grows the City, 1939
Merry Hall, 1951
Laughter on the Stairs, 1953
Beverley Nichols' Cat Book [1955]
Sunlight on the Lawn, 1956
Beverley Nichols' Cats' A. B. C., 1960
Beverley Nichols' Cats' X. Y. Z., 1961
Foreword to Jan Styczynski's *Cats in Camera,* 1962
Garden Open Today, 1963
Garden Open Tomorrow, 1968
Foreword to Orbis's *All About Cats,* 1975

BEVERLEY NICHOLS'

Cats'
A.B.C.

Illustrated by Derrick Sayer

JONATHAN CAPE

THIRTY BEDFORD SQUARE · LONDON

TYPE SET BY THE ALDEN PRESS (OXFORD) LTD
PRINTED IN GREAT BRITAIN BY
LOWE & BRYDONE (PRINTERS) LTD, LONDON
BOUND BY A. W. BAIN & CO. LTD, LONDON

Author's Note

I have no great fondness for the common expression 'cat-lover'. It suggests that he is a strange, cranky person with exclusively feline affections. I am a 'cat-lover', but I am also devoted to dogs, to large shaggy horses, Shetland ponies, cockatoos, budgerigars, penguins, furry caterpillars, squirrels, tortoises and tropical fish. Indeed, I have much in common with Noel Coward, to whom I once introduced my first Siamese cat with the words 'I hope you don't mind cats.' Whereupon he bent down, lifted the beautiful creature into his arms, and retorted 'My dear Beverley, I adore all animals to such an extent that I cannot see a water-bison without bursting into tears.'

Therefore throughout these pages for 'cat-lover' or 'non-cat-lover' I have substituted 'F' or 'non-F', indicating a person who is basically feline or non-feline by nature. I do indeed believe that most persons can be divided into these two categories, and that the true F, whether he  is considering the arts, the sciences, or the men and women in the street, will know by instinct when he is in the presence of a kindred spirit. He will recognize, for example, that Rubens was F whereas Rembrandt was not. I mention these universal geniuses to show that Fness is not to be regarded as a measure of greatness but as a quality of the mind. Thus, Fragonard is F, Boucher non-F; Hogarth is F, Goya non-F. Perhaps Fness, or its opposite, is easiest to detect in music. A single cadenza of Chopin, a simple silver phrase of Mozart, a sigh from the lips of Delius ... these are enough to prove their Fness. Whereas one has only to play four bars of a Bach fugue, or glance at the melodic line of a Beethoven bagatelle, to be convinced of their profound non-Fness.

The true F, as he reviews life from this standpoint, will be obliged to ask himself a number of searching questions. Why is it, for example, that so few royalties are ever F? There has not been a truly F monarch in Britain since Charles II. Some superficial historians might claim a degree of Fness for Queen Victoria, but this would almost certainly be due to her devotion to Disraeli, who was flamboyantly F, and her hatred of Gladstone, who was doggedly — in every sense of the word — non-F. And why should men working in the same period and in the same medium so instantly invoke a sense of Fness or its reverse? Thus — Thackeray — F, Dickens — non-F; Maugham — F, Shaw — non-F; Epstein — F, Henry Moore — non-F; Sir Thomas Beecham — F, Sir Malcolm Sargent — non-F; Greta Garbo — F, Danny Kaye and Marlene Dietrich — non-F; Arthur Miller — F, John Osborne — non-F; Nye Bevan — F, Mr Gaitskell — non-F.

Why, again, should we be obliged, at times, to award the accolade of Fness to persons from whom we should much prefer to withhold it? Reluctant though we may be to admit it, Mr Krushchev is strongly F, though of course a very regrettable scratchy sort of F, whose nature has been warped by evil company and an unnatural existence. And so was Karl Marx — an admission which surely goes to prove the complete impartiality of the present writer. However, we are not concerned with the exceptional genius but with the common reader. F or non-F, I hope that he may find a few moments of diversion in the following pages.

B. (F) N.

Acknowledgments

My thanks are due to the following for permission to quote the verses included in this book: the Author's Representative and Sidgwick & Jackson Ltd for the extract from 'Dining-Room Tea' from *Collected Poems of Rupert Brooke*; the Trustees of the Hardy Estate and Macmillan & Co., Ltd for two verses from 'Lines to a Dumb Friend' by Thomas Hardy from *Collected Poems*; The Cresset Press for the lines from 'To a Caged Lion' by Ruth Pitter from her book *On Cats*; and Chapman and Grimes Inc., Boston, U.S.A., for the verse by Muriel Schulz quoted on page 101 — this is from their publication *Sophisti-Cats*, compiled and edited by Lynn Hamilton.

Because of her feline grace
and subtle understanding
I dedicate this book to

CHRISTABEL,
LADY ABERCONWAY

who
has supremely merited
the honour of being entitled
a Cat

A stands for Amusements.

We must be brutally frank, from the very outset, about the whole business of playing with cats and kittens. Many persons who think themselves impeccably F have in fact little understanding of it.

Let us take as a simple example the familiar device of a length of string to which we attach a screwed-up piece of paper, in order to simulate a mouse. A regrettably large proportion of cat-owners, having manufactured this elementary form of diversion, seem to imagine that nothing remains to be done but to drag the string languidly across the carpet, giving it an occasional twitch, while the cat or kitten leaps and pounces and cavorts in its wake.

This is surely the most stingy and unimaginative behaviour; it is totally lacking in drama, and drama is the essence of all feline diversion. Even as he ties the paper to the string the cat-owner should become tense, his fingers should tremble slightly, and he should cast occasional sidelong glances towards the cat, who will be regarding him with cool concentration, appraising his performance. (All cats are dramatic critics, just as all dramatic critics are cats.)

The device completed, a few final moments of psychological 'conditioning' are advisable. Holding the string in his hands the true F should say to himself: 'I am no longer the owner of a pleasing furry quadruped, who is about to romp round the room. I am now in actual fact a mouse.' Whereupon he must shrink, and shrink, and go on shrinking, with increasing alarm, transmitting his emotions down the string as though it were a telegraph wire, until the paper at the other end is impregnated with his personality. He may then, in a mouse-like manner, twitch the string, at the same time closing his eyes, gritting his teeth and awaiting the Pounce of Doom.

(Practical Note. While these manœuvres are *en train* it is as well to lock the door. To be suddenly wrenched back into the world of humans, when one has successfully shrunk, is most disturbing to the nervous system.)

All is now in readiness for the actual performance. This is best given in a large house, where there is a wide staircase, so that the string may be trailed up and down, step by step, and occasionally swung through the banisters. All cats have a curious passion for banisters, and some of the pleasantest moments in my life have been spent pushing little pieces of paper, feathers, pencils and such-like through the banisters of an old Georgian house, for the delectation of 'One',[1] my first Siamese — now, alas, departed from this world.

Talking of 'One' reminds me of a favourite diversion of all Siamese cats, which seems to be little known even in the best F circles ...

[1] For an explanation of the numerical names of my cats, please turn to page 70.   B. N.

Backsliding. I discovered this by accident. One winter evening 'One' was lying on his back enjoying the warmth of a blazing log fire. His front legs were stretched out at full length behind him, his head lolled to one side, and though at first he seemed to be asleep he was in fact regarding me out of the corner of one blue eye. It was, in short, an attitude of allurement, but I could not interpret it. What was required? Tummy-rubbing? Chin-stroking? Neither of these seemed to meet the case. Then I put my hand on his chest and gave him a slight push backwards. Immediately his eyes opened and he registered an expression of delight. I pushed again, a little farther. The delight increased to ecstasy, and he remained on his back, with his paws dangling in front of him. So I increased the pressure, crawling on my knees beside him, pushing him backwards against the pile of the carpet. Every time that I paused for lack of breath he stayed stock still, demanding more.

Presumably the sensation of the carpet rubbing against his spine was like a sort of super-stroke. Whatever the reason, it became a 'must' in 'One's' programme of amusement. As time went on we became increasingly expert, and since we both had implicit trust in one another, the Backsliding developed many brilliant variations — under the piano, and through the legs of chairs. It was even practised in the kitchen, which was covered with linoleum, so that 'One' could be catapulted across it for distances of up to ten feet.

I should hesitate to publish this diversion to the world without the accompanying diagram, which shows the correct position in which the hand should be placed. If it is too high, pussy will choke; if it is too low, no proper balance can be achieved, and pussy will give the same sort of dirty look as I once observed on the face of a famous ballerina, when her partner was fiddling about with the wrong part of her waist during a difficult passage of *Swan Lake*. And even with the diagram, another word of warning must be spoken. Elderly Siamese cats, who have graced households where Backsliding is not practised, may — on a first introduction — be puzzled and even faintly outraged if one attempts to explain it to them. So, indeed, may their owners. More than one foolish woman, on seeing me initiate her pet in this charming pastime, has protested that I am hurting pussy, or frightening her, or some such grotesque suggestion. But if I am only given one minute — no more — in which to explain the elements, even the most respectable dowager Siamese will succumb, and will recline in the centre of the Aubusson, paws dangling, asking … no, positively demanding … that the Backsliding should continue.

Backsliding, as we have observed, is almost exclusively a Siamese taste; the average tabby will have none of it. Even the gentlest attempt to teach the elements of Backsliding to the ordinary cat is doomed to failure. Pussy will curl into a protesting ball of fur, and if the worst comes to the worst, pussy will scratch.

Most feline amusements, such as ping-pong balls, are enjoyed by every variety of cat. For example, I have yet to meet the cat which does not throw itself whole-heartedly into the Newspaper Game. This requires two or more players — perhaps the ideal number is three — and no apparatus except a few sheets of newspaper. Any newspaper will do, though my own cats, who are inclined to be choosy, seem to prefer the *Financial Times*. The procedure is simple. The largest and most docile of the players is placed in the centre of the carpet, and gently covered with a sheet of newspaper. If the newspaper does not entirely cover the cat, a second sheet may be added, so that pussy is completely invisible with the exception of the tip of her tail. It is important that this should remain uncovered.

'But this is absurd!' the non-F may exclaim. 'Covering an animal with a newspaper and expecting it to stay still! Who ever heard of such a

thing? If I were to try such tricks with my dog … ' To which I would retort: 'We are not suggesting that this game should be played with dogs. Nor with elephants nor with eagles. But it can, and should, be played with cats … with all cats, that is to say, who have been treated as equals, if not as superiors.'

This may be a strange fact, but it is a fact. Covered by her canopy of the *Financial Times*, pussy remains as still as a graven image. The other players may now be placed in strategic positions. For a few moments there will be silence and an atmosphere of unbearable tension. Then the pussy under the newspaper gives a sharp twitch with her tail, indicating that she is ready. Whereupon, almost immediately, one of the players will pounce, and the game has begun. Experienced pouncers will probably land on the edge of the newspaper, and then beat a rapid retreat. Sometimes they may not pounce at all, preferring to stalk and dab, in the manner of matadors. Kittens usually pounce rather too soon, and sometimes, not quite getting the hang of it, they push their noses under the paper and are pounced on in their turn. But if the game is skilfully played, with suitable co-operation from the cat-owner in the matter of readjusting the newspaper when it slips off pussy's back, it will provide moments of the greatest excitement, and by the end of it the room will be littered with scraps of newspaper and Gaskin will have to come in with the Hoover.

Strange as it may seem — or is it so strange? — many cats greatly enjoy taking part in games which are usually regarded as for humans only, such as playing patience. I play a great deal of patience during my work, usually about six games to the morning; when one's invention is flagging a game of patience is like a pause by the wayside to regain one's wind. In these games I am greatly assisted — though perhaps that is not quite the word — by 'Five', particularly if he has just come in from the garden with muddy paws. Indeed, 'Five' has left so many paw-prints on my various packs of cards that I am able to cheat with comparative ease.

Then there is that very soothing game called Scrabble. My cat Oscar is a keen Scrabble player. This game, in my house, is conducted on a large circular Regency table with a glass top, and as soon as Oscar hears the clatter of the counters he leaps on to the table, eager to join the party. Normally he keeps his enthusiasm within bounds, contenting himself with an occasional dab at the pool of counters, which sends a few of them on to the floor. There have been occasions, however, when he is less restrained, and attacks the board itself. I shall never forget the time when a somewhat frenzied female guest, at the end of the game, had triumphantly placed the letter Z on a treble square, and having done so, proceeded to add the letters ITH. But that was as far as she got. For Oscar, misinterpreting her gestures, chose that moment to give the board a sharp swipe, which scattered the whole pattern in hopeless confusion. 'That monstrous cat of yours!' cried the lady. 'It was going to have been ZITHER and it would have been a treble and it would have won me the game.' I pointed out that it would, in fact, have done nothing of the sort, for the letters ZI would have clashed with the letters QU in the next row, and there was, as far as I was aware, no word even remotely resembling ZIQU in current use in the English language. (After a long course of Scrabble, and a great deal of reference to the *Oxford Dictionary*, I am not so sure about that last remark. I should not be surprised to look up ZIQU and find that it was, in fact, a rare but amiable form of antelope, native of Formosa.)

Perhaps you do not play Scrabble. In which case I fear that this story will have bored you. So let us leave the house and wander into the garden.

I often think that the ideal setting for outdoor feline sport is the orchard. (Except during the months of September and October, when the grass is scattered with windfalls. For with the windfalls come the wasps, and there have been occasions when pussy has sniffed a wasp, with disastrous and melodramatic results.) But if it is the month of May, when the blossom is out, and if one is accompanied by a white Persian kitten, which allows itself to be lifted on to a lower branch, in order to dab at twigs, moments of the utmost enchantment are almost certain to ensue. There is only one disadvantage to this pastime. The kitten is so exquisite, the apple-blossom is so liltingly beautiful, the white clouds scudding across the sky are so charged with the winds of poetry, the whole design, in short, is so stunningly photogenic — including, one trusts, one's own profile in the bottom left-hand corner — that one feels self-conscious, as though one were posing for the cover of a Christmas calendar. Which, now I come to think of it, might not be such a bad idea.

B stands for Beeing.

The spelling will explain itself in a moment. For B also stands for beetling and butterflying. And for a great many other things which do not begin with B, such as hedgehogging, and dragonflying and spidering and goldfishing and — though it sounds almost unbearably whimsical — for daddy long-legging, or as the Germans might say, *grossvaterbeinenspiel*. And — here we heave a sigh — B also stands for mousing.

The problem of the cat and the mouse is one that has been argued between Fs and non-Fs since time immemorial. The non-Fs cite it as one of the reasons why they dislike cats. Whereupon, the Fs feel very uncomfortable and try to gloss over the subject with vague references to 'Nature'.

Personally I should have thought that this was one of those problems which might reasonably be deposited, fairly and squarely, on the lap of the Almighty, who — with all deference — can hardly evade all responsibility. However, before doing so, let us consider a few facts. Let us clear our minds by studying the behaviour of my own cats, 'Four', 'Five' and Oscar.

Never was there a less bloodthirsty trio. Perhaps it would be unbecoming of me to suggest that this may be because they have inherited some of the amiable characteristics of their master. (The only blood-sport in which I ever indulge is Flitting Flies and even then I have some qualms of conscience, particularly in the case of very large black flies that refuse to swoon swiftly away, but lie buzzing on their backs and then suddenly get up again and swoop dizzily across to the other end of the room. For this reason I usually supplement the Flit gun with a whisk, in order to ensure a speedy dispatch.)

But though my cats are exceptionally unpredatory, they *are* cats, with the instinct of hunting, which must have an occasional outlet. But instead of chasing mice, rats or any of the conventional quarries, they usually choose very different objects. Hence the expression — Beeing.

Beeing was invented by 'Five', in the days when I had a large bed of heather outside the window of my music room. 'Five' used to play in this heather when he was a kitten; it was a lovely place for bouncing about on, like an immense feather bed; and some of it was tall enough for him to imagine that he was in a jungle. Then one day in early spring the sun came out hot and strong, and since there was still plenty of *erica carnea* in flower, the bees arrived in hosts. They went to 'Five's' head in more senses than one, but fortunately we had somebody staying who understood the technique  of sting-removing and of bathing 'the affected part' with bicarbonate of soda. As time went on, 'Five' became more cunning. He treated the bees rather as though they were tennis balls being sent over the net by a pro, sitting quite still and giving them an occasional sharp bash with a closed paw, which sent them reeling indignantly into a mound of pink blossom. Stings were few and far between. All the same, whenever 'Five' stalked out to his vantage point in the heather I would send a warning message to Gaskin: ' "Five" is Beeing, be ready with the bicarbonate.'

Now consider 'Four'. He has no feeling about bees at all. Even if you were to sit him in front of a large snapdragon when immense bumble-bees were pushing their gold-dusted bottoms through the velvet curtains — like very fat ladies negotiating revolving doors — 'Four' would be quite unmoved. For 'Four' is almost exclusively a fisherman.

In every garden I have ever owned there has been a lily pond, for a garden without water is like a room without a looking glass; the sheet of water, even if it is only a tiny one, seems to smile up to the sky, and the sky smiles back, and there you are, with a little patch of heaven on the lawn. But by the side of this patch of heaven, unfortunately, there is usually to be found a small black imp, fishing. 'Four' practises this art with skill and intelligence. He has learned how to place himself so that his shadow does not fall athwart the water. He has also learned that there are certain clumps of water grasses which conceal him from detection by anybody looking through the windows of the house. He sits stock-still — not even the twitch of a tail. In spite of this, he seldom catches anything, and I could count on the fingers of one hand the occasions when a small, golden, and rather gruesome corpse has been deposited outside the back door as a proof of his prowess.

As for Oscar — he is primarily a bird-watcher, with the accent very much on the word 'watching'. He sits at the window making the most grue-some castanet noises with his teeth. If looks could kill there would not be a sparrow left in Surrey. Every time I see this savage demeanour

18

I am reminded of a certain performance of *Norma* at La Scala in Milan, with Callas in the leading role. I watched this charming old *marron glacé* of an opera from a box in which I was flanked by two rival prima donnas. At the ovation which greeted the end of the aria 'Carta Diva' the faces of these two ladies wore expressions exactly like Oscar's when he is bird-watching; they were contorted with rage and envy and the most fiendish malice; and if Madame Callas had been a bird, her days would have been short indeed.

But the mouse is waiting, as it were, in the wings, the symbol of the eternal argument between Fs and non-Fs. I suggested above that this was a problem which might be deposited in the lap of the Almighty, like all other problems involving the basic sin of cruelty. If this sounds to the non-F as though I were evading the issue, let me suggest that we send it instead to the members of the Loamshire Stag-Hunting Association, or some similar collection of primitive barbarians. Stag-hunting is a purely human pastime. It is carried on, with the hysterical co-operation of hounds — 'dogs are so much more sporting than cats!' — solely for the purpose of amusement. It has not the primary excuse, which can be made for all animals, that its members are obeying an ancient instinct that compels them to kill in order to eat. It is cruelty, naked and unadorned, and before the non-F begins to attack pussy for chasing her mouse, I would suggest that he began to put his own human house in order.

All the same, on the very rare occasions when my own cats discover a mouse, there is an immediate crisis, a frenzied rushing hither and thither and an appalling expenditure of nervous energy.

How do *you* deal with a mouse crisis? What do you do if you suddenly look out of the window and see, to your

dismay, that It has happened again ... that pussy is doing this terrible *danse macabre* on the lawn, pouncing and retreating and cavorting? (Though I appear to be censuring pussy I cannot refrain from reminding non-Fs that her demeanour, even in such moments, contrasts very favourably with that of Salome.)

My own actions depend entirely on whether Gaskin is in or out. If he is in I rush to the kitchen and break the news. 'Four' has a mouse. It is on the lawn. It is in the shrubbery. Or worst of all, it is actually being transported towards the back door. Does Gaskin think that he could possibly ... ? Gaskin sighs, wipes his hands, folds up a dishcloth, takes a small frying-pan from the rack, and departs, to deal with the situation. Five minutes later he returns, having dealt with it. The mouse has escaped. No, it was *not* hurt and 'Four' has been shut up in the toolshed to calm down. Or the mouse was already dead, and partially devoured, and 'Four' will almost certainly be sick. (Serve him right, one thinks.) Or the mouse was alive, but swiftly dispatched with the frying-pan.

After which, the household gradually reverts to normal.

If Gaskin is out, things are not so easy. I should be little use with the frying-pan, though in the last extremity I might resort to it. And so my principal weapon is vocal. Yells and roars and shouts and imprecations, as I chase pussy across the lawn or through the shrubbery. In any ordinary household these tactics might not work. But my cats are so used to deference, they are so accustomed to gentle accents, that when they suddenly see me rushing after them, bellowing like a bull, they experience a shock of such acute astonishment that the mouse is usually abandoned. Which means, of course, that one crisis is immediately supplanted by another. For though the mouse is saved, pussy has fled in alarm, and one is immediately haunted by the thought that she has gone for good, and has set out on some lonely, fateful journey through the lanes and the hedgerows where she will eventually starve to death. These are times when I think it would be really much less exhausting to keep tortoises.

Only once did the vocal tactics cause embarrassment. The mouser was Oscar and Gaskin was not at hand. I shot out, as usual, roaring and cursing, while Oscar carried out evasive tactics in the hedge. 'Put it down!' I yelled. Bellow, bellow, bellow. 'Stop it at once!' Bang, bang, bang with a brick on the frying-pan. 'Put that wretched thing *down*!' Unfortunately the hedge skirted a lane down which, at that very moment, the ladies of the local Conservative Association were marching, grim-faced, on their way to a meeting at the village hall. They were carrying a blue banner embroidered with the words For Queen and Country. They misinterpreted my action and I was never asked to open their garden fête again.

stands for Cuisine.

Every pussy, if given a chance, is an epicure. The pussy who has been brought up with love and understanding never gobbles her food, and though on rising from the table she may not send her compliments to the chef in so many words, she makes it very clear if she has been pleased or not. Even non-Fs will agree that this demeanour is in striking contrast to the behaviour of dogs, who gulp their meals in a grossly animal manner, and very seldom complain even if they are offered the sort of fare which used to be provided on British Railways. In which their conduct strikingly resembles that of their masters.

My own cats have always been fortunate in the fact they they have been served by a first-class chef in the form of Gaskin. He takes as much trouble with their meals as with mine, and would be distressed if their whiting were not *à point* as if my *soufflé* had failed to rise. I need hardly say that in the course of twenty-five years neither of these disasters has yet occurred.

Moreover, Gaskin takes almost as much trouble with what might be called the general arrangements of the table as with the actual preparation of the dishes. Thus, he regards placing as of vital importance. Many of us have probably attended dinner parties in Paris where there have been frightful *froideurs* about procedure, when some obscure but legitimate count has threatened to leave the room because he has been placed in an inferior position to an equally obscure, but bastard, marquis. Throughout history, members of the French aristocracy have always been so busy fussing about where they sit at table that they usually have failed to notice that the entire country is sinking rapidly into the abyss. Gaskin's seating arrangements for the pussies arise from no such foolish snobbishness; he has merely learned, from long experience, that there are certain places where they like to dine and certain places where they do not, and that is that. Why they have chosen these places, nobody knows, and as far as I am aware, nobody has ever been so vulgar as to ask them.

Thus, 'Four' insists on breakfasting under the kitchen sink, 'Five' on the kitchen table, and Oscar in a corner by the side of the dresser. Were the plates to be placed in any other position, they would be ignored. There would be pained expressions, lashings of the tail, shruggings of the shoulders, and exits into the garden, and no food would be partaken until Gaskin had come to his senses.

This fastidiousness has its drawbacks. There have been a few unhappy occasions when I have been abroad, and when Gaskin has gone away for the night. Needless to say, before doing so he has engaged a reliable woman as a 'temporary' to attend to the cats' menus. He has inquired into her antecedents, vetted her character, and thoroughly coached her in the technique. The fish must be cooked just so long, and no more. The milk must be warmed. There must be a large bowl of fresh water. The times for breakfast and dinner must be strictly observed; 7.45 for breakfast, 4.15 for dinner. Above all, the position of the plates must never vary ... 'Four' under the sink, 'Five' on the kitchen table, and

Oscar by the dresser. 'You understand?' says Gaskin. Yes, says the temporary, she understands. Whereupon Gaskin, with a last beetling glance, hands her the latchkey and departs, not without forebodings.

Alas, the forebodings have sometimes been justified. Even reliable women, with clean aprons and rosy faces, may have a sinister streak of non-Fness in their characters. Such a one was Mrs ... never mind, we will call her Mrs X. How was Gaskin to know that Mrs X, who had impeccable references, with duchesses raving about her *soufflés* across pages of coroneted writing paper, could possibly be so wickedly incompetent about feeding the cats? No — it was not incompetence, it was done with deliberation. For Mrs X, arriving on the following morning in the empty house — admittedly on time — suddenly decided that the cats were 'pampered'. (In subsequent cross-examination she actually *confessed* to this.) And so, having cooked the fish, she set it all on a large plate in the centre of the floor and left the cats to it, under the astonishing impression that they would eat it. She had some odd, barbaric notion that she was 'teaching them a lesson'. I am not suggesting that she was actually a sadist, and I believe that she was quite a good mother to her own three very plain and sniffly children who would probably have eaten with the greatest relish off a communal plate in the middle of the floor. All the same, I really do think it a great pity that there should be such women in the world.

24

Cats, of course, have exquisite table manners, though their etiquette differs somewhat from the more restricted human variety. I wonder if any of the following customs are shared by the pets of other Fs?

1. Dabbing. This is permissible in the best circles. My own principal dabber is 'Five'. He usually decides to dab when offered a small piece of the dish one is eating oneself. He enters the dining-room, sits by one's chair, and subjects one to a steady stare. Needless to say, he would never do anything so impolite as to mew, or to reach up to the table. The stare is duly rewarded by a small portion of chicken or steak or whatever one may be eating. This is cut up, as a *bonne bouche*, and placed before him. Whereupon 'Five' lowers his head and contemplates the *bonne bouche*. This contemplation may last for several minutes. 'Really, "Five", you are a spoilt cat,' one says. 'That is a beautiful piece of chicken. There are many cats, sleeping on the Embankment, who would be most grateful for ... ' But one does not finish the sentence, for if one begins to think of cats sleeping on the Embankment one will have a wretched night and get no sleep oneself. However, the reproof seems to have registered, for 'Five' suddenly emerges from contemplation and gives the piece of chicken a sharp dab with his right paw. It slides to the edge of the plate; then it is dabbed back again with the left paw. For all I know, this may be 'Five's' retort to one's remark about the Embankment; it may be his way of saying that such painful subjects should not be mentioned at meal times. Whatever the reason, he eventually eats the pieces of chicken. Having done so, he sits down and makes his toilet. He never asks for more.

2. Growling. This habit may seem to non-Fs to conflict with the claim for 'exquisite table manners'. I do not think so, for two reasons. Firstly, because there is only one dish — at least as far as my own cats are concerned — which gives rise to growling ... rabbit. Why this should be, I do not pretend to understand. I can only register the fact that when

rabbit is on the menu, growls are in the air. They are very fierce growls, accompanied by dramatic movements of the head over the shoulder, as though seeking some imaginary enemy.

The other reason why I am, as it were, pro-growling, is because I think it would greatly enliven human dinner parties if it were generally adopted. I would not growl over most of the dishes one is offered in British households, but I would certainly growl over caviare. If one is the least important guest, as one usually is, and if one is sitting in Starvation Corner, and if one sees great dollops of this ambrosia being ladled out to fat rich ladies who could well afford to buy it by the bucket, and if one is eventually given a tiny reluctant scraping from the bottom of the jar ... surely one *should* growl? One should not only growl, but scratch and pounce and hiss. One does, in spirit, but not in fact, and repression, as we all know, ties the psyche up in knots.

3. Leaving a small piece uneaten. All delicately nurtured felines do this. It is the ultimate proof of good breeding. Even if one adopts the scruffiest alley cat, as soon as he has been plumped out and given the blessed assurance that his days of scrummaging in dustbins are over, he will leave a little bit of dinner uneaten. I have never known any exceptions to this rule. It is absoutely *de rigueur*, and it suggests that somewhere, in the Feline Archives, there must be some venerated volume of Etiquette. for Cats, thumbed by countless paws and sniffed over by hosts of little noses, whose lessons are passed down from generation to generation.

26

D stands for Dilapidations.

If Oscar were a human I should send him a small bill for the current year. It would be made out as follows:

To re-upholstering two armchairs
covered in primrose yellow silk
repp   £22 os. od.

To repairing back of one Chippendale settee in antique
crimson brocade   £15 os. od.

To relaying lower steps of staircase carpet and replacing with
strips of new material   £18 os. od.

To patching various portions of
music-room curtains in yellow
velvet   £12 os. od.

To supplying new silk fringes for
pair of large settees   £9 os. od.

To sundry scratches all over the
house   £10 os. od.
                                        _____

                                        £86 os. od.
                                        _____

It may seem ungracious — even non-F — to mention such matters in public. But though eighty-six pounds would be a small sum to pay for all the pleasure which Oscar gives me, year by year, these items do mount up. And since this is a severely practical handbook, as you will have observed, the problem of pussy's claws must be faced, honestly and objectively.

The first thing to be noted is that the only chair-scratcher is Oscar. 'Four' never scratches a thing. 'Five' occasionally *assumes* the attitude of scratching, standing on his hind legs and placing his front paws firmly on a piece of new brocade. But then he pauses, turns his head, and catches one's eye. Whereupon, with an air of elaborate insouciance, he withdraws his paws, as though he had been merely smoothing out a wrinkle in the brocade. As a final proof that he thinks the whole thing grossly exaggerated, he yawns and stalks away.

But Oscar is shameless. He is a very large and very beautiful cat, with claws like sabres, and he seems positively to enjoy this supreme naughtiness. In the full light of day, under one's very nose, he will stalk over to the divan, eye it carefully, prepare to scratch, extend his claws, and drag them down. And one more scar is left on the primrose yellow silk repp, which was over two pounds a yard (single width).

Does this mean that Oscar is a sadist? Is there some obscure Jack-the-Ripper streak in him? Shall we wake up one day and see his whiskers plastered all over the front page of the *News of the World*?

No. Oscar's trouble is simply one of an unfortunate environment in his youth. It is on a par with the problems of most juvenile delinquents who have come from unsuitable homes. Unlike 'Four' and 'Five', whose early attempts at scratching were gently but firmly discouraged by giving them taps on their paws with a folded newspaper, Oscar was actually encouraged in his naughtiness. His original owner was a Chelsea artist who lived in a studio of quite exceptional squalor. Nothing was ever dusted, nothing was ever washed up, and the remains of ancient meals lingered on in odd corners for days. In this excessively Bohemian atmo-sphere, where most of the furniture had been purchased off pavements in Chelsea and brought home in a barrow, Oscar could scratch to his heart's content. Shouts of laughter greeted his assaults as he tore the last few pieces of sack-cloth off a chair with broken springs. And bets were taken on him when he began to climb the curtains.

Then the artist decided to live abroad and

Oscar, the Cockney ragamuffin, was given a new home at Merry Hall. 'What "Four" and "Five" will say I do *not* know!' observed Gaskin, in the grimmest tones. What they said will have to wait for another chapter.

Now Merry Hall was not so grand as all that, but compared with the studio it was the South Kensington Museum, the Wallace Collection, and then some. Oscar, after he had found his way around, and finished his conversations with 'Four' and 'Five' — which lasted for several days — proceeded to go about the congenial task of tearing it to pieces. At first we did not take him too seriously. 'He will soon learn,' we said optimistically, as we tapped his paws with the newspaper. 'It will not be long before he comes under the good influence of "Four" and "Five".' But he did not learn. And far from coming under the influence of 'Four' and 'Five', there were sinister signs that he might actually begin to corrupt them also. I noticed strange, frustrated gleams in their eyes as they sat and watched his forbidden activities.

What could one do? As time went on, and as more and more furniture was torn to pieces, I asked myself if there was any material which was scratch-proof. I made inquiries at various shops, and was shown several fabrics guaranteed to resist damage, but most of them looked as if they had been designed for use in homes for juvenile delinquents. Besides, I was attached to my silk repp; moreover, I had paid for it ... heavily.

Was there anything one could spray on — any sort of deterrent? For a short while there was a period of hope. A friend brought from Paris a large box of powder which was called something like Contre-Chat. I did not much care for having such a thing about the house; the idea of being *contre-chat*, even in such an emergency, was naturally distressing. However, the situation was getting desperate; the furniture in the music-room was disintegrating before my very eyes, and we had long passed the stage where Oscar's assaults could be concealed by clipping off pieces of frayed silk with a pair of nail-scissors. And so, with some reluctance — and concealing the offending title from Oscar's interested eyes — I went into the music-room and sprinkled the powder all over Oscar's favourite pieces. I noticed, as I did so, that it had a strong scent of moth-balls. 'And now, Oscar,' I observed coldly, 'you will have to sit on the floor.' But Oscar did nothing of the sort. The powder had no effect on him. It had, however, a considerable effect on me, and even more on my friends. An overpowering scent of naphthalene is not a social asset.

Then there was the episode of the 'Scratching Tree'. This I discovered one Christmas, in the animal shop of a large London store, where I had dropped in to have a few words with an extremely beguiling macaw. The tree was a log about three feet high, mounted on a wooden base, and the young lady assured me that all cats were mad about it, and would scratch it to death, ignoring all one's 'choicer pieces' (her phrase, not mine.) So I bought it and took it home, and for about twenty-four hours it was a wild success, and the choicer pieces were left in peace. Admittedly, a large log standing bolt upright next to a Queen Anne chair looked rather peculiar, but one could always push it behind a screen if anybody called. If there was not time to do so, one could pretend that one was interested in modern sculpture, and say that it was a statue of Maternity, by the new genius Catacat.

However, the charm of the Scratching Tree was short-lived. By the following evening the choicer pieces were being subjected to fresh assaults.

This was really impossible. There was only one thing to be done. I must harden my heart. Oscar's claws must be cut. The vet. must be summoned without a moment's delay. I went to the telephone and lifted the receiver ...

This, as I have observed before, is a sternly practical volume, in which no trace of whimsy must be allowed to intrude. I have hopes that it will eventually take its place on the library shelves of veterinary surgeons, who will turn to it in moments of obstetric emergency, when they are in doubt as to some detail of technique.

At the same time I must permit myself just one moment of light relief to tell you about Oscar having his claws cut.

He lay back, green-eyed, purring, stretched out on my lap. 'Pretty pussy, pretty pussy,' murmured the vet. or words to that effect. Oscar raised his eyebrows. This was curiously adolescent conversation, he seemed to be saying. However ... He extended his paw. He seemed to know all about it. There was a clip, and another clip. I held my breath. This was going far better than I had dared to hope. 'There! That's one paw done!' said the vet. But no. Oscar ... as though he were reclining in a chair in a very grand barber's shop, yawned, drew back his paw, examined it, and extended it again. He was not satisfied. 'Dear me,' said the vet. 'I have forgotten the side claw.' Whereupon Oscar emitted a faint, smug purr.

In short, Oscar actually enjoyed having his claws cut. And I believe that your cat would like having his claws cut too.

BUT ... and I will write the word in capital letters, because it is a very big BUT ... please remember this vital point about claw-cutting.

It should never be done at all if you live in an area where pussy is likely to encounter dogs. You will be sending him defenceless into the world. He will be unable to hit back, unable to climb to any place of refuge, and you will be guilty of the grossest cruelty.

You may ask ... what about Oscar? Well, Oscar's area is a large country garden, surrounded by vine-clad walls and twisted hedges, and since only his front claws are cut, leaving his back ones intact, he can still scramble to safety in comparative comfort. Apart from that, there only seem to be two dogs within reasonable distance, both of them aged, corpulent and of apparently pacific dispositions. If anything large, fierce and black were suddenly to appear next door, the whole situation would have to be drastically reviewed.

Finally, let me repeat that there should never be the least need for claw-cutting if pussy has been properly brought up as a kitten. A few gentle taps with a newspaper, from time to time, should cure scratching for good and all.

E stands for Elegance.

As each year goes by the delicate word 'elegance' — so prettily shaved and with such appealing echoes — becomes more nearly obsolete, or perhaps one should say more exclusively applicable to the past. I have read, for example, a great many articles in praise of modern furniture. I have been informed that a square of orange sackcloth, supported on four hair-pin legs, with a triangular back of the same material ... I refer, of course, to the modern chair ... is 'exciting', 'streamlined to the contemporary trend' and 'the epitome of modern living'. All these things I can well believe, though I am not quite certain what they mean. I would merely reply, with the utmost courtesy, mumbling through my senile jaws, that if this is indeed the epitome of modern living I would greatly prefer to die.

Consider only one of the objects which are apparently regarded as essential to 'exciting', 'streamlined' modern living — the ubiquitous rubber plant. If you turn over the pages of any magazine devoted to interior decoration you will find one advertisement after another featuring this regrettable vegetable. Sometimes it is placed on the chimney piece under a reproduction of a nude by Matisse — (five guineas, including frame). Sometimes it is bang in the middle of the dining-table, which in itself is enough to give one both cramp and indigestion, being so stream-lined that there is no room for one's legs, and fashioned from a peculiarly repellent variety of wood that should have been left to wilt in the jungles of Peru instead of being brought over to warp in the jungles of Peckham. Strangest of all the rubber plant is frequently placed in the nursery, where contemporary streamlined infants are depicted playing on eye-aching rugs imported from Sweden … I never really trusted the Swedes … while Mummy and Daddy recline on a super-modern settee that looks as though it has been designed as a couch for a particularly evil sort of osteopath.

From these observations, which have been written with such iron restraint that my back aches, you may have gathered that I am not an admirer of modern furniture.

And you may well be asking what on earth all this has to do with cats. Just this. Cats are the most elegant of all God's creatures. As soon as a cat walks into a modern room the whole vulgar collection of 'stream-lined' bits and pieces looks even more gauche and shoddy than before. Cats were created to recline on chairs by Chippendale, or perhaps one should say that chairs by Chippendale were created for cats to recline on. Their milk should be poured from jugs of Queen Anne silver, and when they walk into the garden they should do so, whenever possible, via a long and lofty Palladian colonnade, with a footman in attendance. It is bitter to realize that these simple conditions in this day and age are so seldom fulfilled.

A word about the practical application of feline elegance.

It has always struck me as extraordinary that cats are not permanently retained, at high fees, in all schools for the training of mannequins and all institutions where models are put through their paces. Before each opening of the spring and autumn collections of Paris the young women who are about to display the dresses should be gathered together, and lined up in a row, while pussy slowly parades before them, to show how it should be done. True, the models would probably all develop violent inferiority complexes, for the woman has yet to be born who can manipulate a train with the same grace as pussy twitching her tail. However, it would be worth the risk.

In particular, pussy's technique of entering a room should be studied by all women who wish to win friends and influence people. Sometimes, on festive occasions, I have been bidden to the Savoy Hotel, which is not an eating-house I normally patronize. As I have a timid disposition and an excess of politeness I always arrive too early, and as there is a limit to the time one can spend straightening one's tie in the gentlemen's lavatory, I invariably find myself secreted behind a potted palm, looking at my wrist-watch, scanning the horizon for my hostess, and wondering when it would be safe to emerge without too much loss of caste. From this vantage-point I have had a rare opportunity to study the exits and entrances of many types of women as they sweep up and down the staircase ... the film stars, the American matrons, the debutantes, and that large reserve of nice women up from the country who always manage to make pink chiffon look like tweed. None of these women could hold a candle to even an alley cat in the matter of poise and deportment. For instance, none of them know how to pause. When pussy pauses, in the middle of a promenade, she automatically freezes into a posture of the utmost grace and for a moment the whole world seems to stop around her. When a woman pauses she merely looks as if something had stuck.

Consider pussy, then, all women who desire to ensnare the male. Consider her as she walks, as she sits, as she rises, as she lays herself down to sleep. You will never emulate her perfection. But with patience and humility and complete obedience to the feline laws you may at least eliminate some of your major faults.

F stands for Fur.

Before we say any more, I would like to observe, in the most dulcet tones, that though I am passionately against the institution of capital punishment, and though I have no liking for the birch as an instrument of correction, there have been moments, of recent years, when I have faintly regretted the abolition of both. These have been when I have read of the activities of the cat thieves. When I think of those sub-human brutes, prowling round the dark alleys, thrusting out a thieving arm to grip somebody's pet round the throat … when I think of the sack, the struggles, the terror, the suffocation … but then, I try not to think of these things, which is weak of me. For if some people had not the courage to endure the torture of thinking of them, there would never be any action.

However, these were meant to be happy pages, so we will send these brutes skulking back into the shadows, with the hope that there may be some special corner of hell reserved for them, in which they will be tied up in sacks, slowly suffocated, and finally skinned to the accompaniment of the Hallelujah Chorus sung by a massed choir of Siamese kittens.

And now for a few thoughts on fur.

At the risk of causing dissension, I must confess that the most *de luxe* form of feline fur, the Persian, is not the variety which affords me, personally, the greatest delight. I see its beauty, I appreciate its miraculous sheen and delicacy, and I need hardly say that when a Persian cat enters the room, with all the glamorous assurance of a film star, I hastily straighten my tie and smooth my hair and click my heels. That is really the trouble — for me — about Persians and their fur. I cannot relax with them. Even when they lie on their backs and demand tummy-rubbing, I feel that I should be taking a liberty if I obeyed their commands — rather as though a glittering prima donna were to sink on to a rich divan, indicating that a moment's dalliance might not be unacceptable. Would not one get all tangled up with tiaras and ostrich-feather capes? I ask only for information; such a situation has not yet arisen in my life, and becomes daily more improbable.

Again, I get worried about fur in the tummy. Not fur in *my* tummy, but in the Persian's. I seem to remember, from the distant past, tales of Persians who had to have balls of fur extracted from them. Then there is the question of lumpiness. Whenever you stroke a Persian — always with this peculiar feeling that you are taking liberties with a prima donna — you come across these lumps. Do they disturb the Persian? Do they keep it awake at nights? Are they being properly attended to? Is some slave with a silver comb perpetually in attendance, with a mirror and a bowl of cream? The answer, in these days of the Welfare State, is probably in the negative. All the best slaves, who ought to be ministering to Persian cats, are almost certainly in the employment of the London County Council, ministering to a lot of nasty little boys and girls.

For this curious complex of reasons, therefore, I have never owned a Persian cat. Or perhaps it would be more fitting to say that I have never been owned by one.

Some cats, as we all know, are born in full evening dress. White shirt, white tie ... (whiskers) ... black tails and all. The illusion is perfect, particularly when they also have smart black paws to match. I love cats in evening dress; they wear it so much more elegantly than we do. Moreover, they never look incongruous in it. There are very few young men

who can sit on a wall in Chelsea, at nine o'clock in the morning, in deep evening dress, delicately scratching their ears, without exciting adverse comment. Indeed, I only knew one, and he came to a bad end. But a great many cats can do it, and always with grace.

Perhaps the most sheerly beautiful of all feline furs is worn by the Siamese. I suppose one would call it beige, but beige has always seemed to me a rather common word, possibly because I knew a very common Australian woman who was always wandering about people's houses, unasked, and telling them that they should have their walls painted beige. She pronounced it 'beeyige' and she made it sound like a sort of cheese. One can't really catalogue the fur of a Siamese; sometimes it is corn-colour, flecked with gold, at others it is old ivory, and there are some very soigné and quite alarmingly distinguished blue points who look as if they had stepped straight out of Lanvin's, who I still think makes the prettiest clothes, whatever anybody may say. And then, of course, the beauty of the Siamese fur is not exactly diminished by the fact that it is always offset by those marvellous brown gloves, those superb stockings, and finally … the jewels of the eyes, which are sapphire or aquamarine or stained-glass-window, according to age and breeding and temperament.

But really it is rather churlish to set one fur against another. There are candle-lit evenings when the fur of my own 'Four' is jet, with a sheen of electric blue; he is the blackest of black pussies but after you have been stroking him for some time this curious and strangely beautiful shade of blue flickers over his back.

And then — what about the fur of tabbies, which affords one of the many proofs that Nature has a sense of humour? My own 'Five' has a smudge on his nose which compels one to think of him as a low comedian. This leads to all sorts of emotional complications. For there are times when 'Five' does not feel in the least like a low comedian, times when he is frightened or bewildered or filled with a nameless *malaise*, times when he is simply sentimental. Whereupon he comes and sits by one's chair and gazes up with those immense green eyes, and one looks down at him with every intention of being emotionally co-operative and adjusting oneself to his mood. But always there is that smudge on the nose and really it is extremely difficult, unless one is a brilliant actor, not to smile at it. Which, of course, would be quite shattering for 'Five', because he would feel that one was making fun of him.

And that leads to yet another reflection. It has nothing to do with F for Fur, but I will set it down while it occurs to me. I am quite certain that all animals who have been domesticated are intensely sensitive to ridicule and sarcasm. To cats ... maybe even more to dogs ... a sneer or a guffaw can be more wounding than a blow. It is a bitter reminder of their 'inferior' status; it sends them back to the darkness of the jungle from which we have taken them.

Not for the first time, I feel thankful that 'Five' cannot read. If he could, and if he chanced upon these pages, I should never be able to look him in the face again.

G stands for Gardening.

All cats are keen gardeners, and in every garden that I have ever made, their shadows lie across the path. Sometimes, I must admit, the garden might have been made more easily without their assistance. Indeed, whenever I think of cats and gardens, I am reminded of the affectionate dedication in one of Mr P. G. Wodehouse's novels ... 'To my dear daughter Leonora, without whose constant advice and encouragement, this book would have been finished in half the time.'

Like their owners, cats soon decide which form of gardening most appeals to them — though none of them, alas, ever takes any interest in weeding. All of them, however, are keen waterers; indeed, they co-operate in this task with such enthusiasm that they lend it an air of drama with which it is not usually associated. If one is using the hose, and if the hose has a leak where it fits on to the tap — and I have yet to meet the hose which has not — pussy feels obliged to investigate this phenomenon, to stalk round it, to put out a tentative paw at the dripping water, to prod it, to frisk round it, and generally to make one feel that something very exciting is occurring — as, of course, it is. When the hose is in action, the drama rises to fresh heights, with pussy lurking behind shrubs (usually in the precise place where one wishes to direct the water) and giving a brilliant histrionic display of alarm. Sometimes, on these occasions, I close my eyes for a moment and try to enter into pussy's mind and I think I can dimly realize how she is feeling. Think of it! One is lurking under a giant tree and across the sky an immense stream of silver is streaking like some fantastic water-spout; there are sounds of thunder as it splashes on the giant leaves and strikes the parched earth; and always there is the shadow of a two-legged monster above one, the Genie of the Waters.

Watering with the can is less emotionally exhausting; indeed I can think of few diversions more soothing, more restful to the soul, than an hour spent in this fashion, on a warm summer evening in an old country garden with a cat in attendance. The fragrance that rises from the grateful earth is like a benison; there is a subtle, shadowy beauty in the darkening soil, a ghostly music in the soft hiss and gurgle of the water. And always of course there is pussy, watching and waiting. There are times, on very hot evenings, when it is permissible to switch the can so that for a second a few drops of water fall across pussy's back. This allows her an opportunity to give a fine display of outraged indignation which leads, in its turn, to a very pleasant scene of reconciliation, with pussy lurking coyly in an inaccessible position under a prickly berberis, while one muddies one's trousers and scratches one's hands trying to coax her out.

There are times — even the most earnest of Fs must admit this — when pussy's gardening activities are more of a hindrance than a help. For example, when seeds have been sown in the open ground, it is discouraging to look out of the window and see that pussy is using the precise place where they are sown as a public convenience. A nice new seed-bed, to pussy, is an immediate reminder that the time has come for washing the hands or powdering the nose; it is almost as though one had stuck a little label into the earth with the word 'Toilette' written in bold black letters.

I really do not quite know how one deals with this problem. No great purpose is served by rushing across the lawn, shooing and clapping one's hands; such a procedure is unfair to pussy and unduly agitating to one's own pulse; besides, by the time one has reached the seed-bed it is probably too late, and one's shilling packet of love-in-the-mist or clarkia or candytuft is scattered to the four winds. One can, of course, protect the seeds with a cloche, but I never much care for cloches in a garden; they are always getting broken and spattered with mud, and they set one's teeth on edge with the noise they make when their edges grate together.

Perhaps the best plan is to adopt the same procedure as we use to keep sparrows off crocuses, i.e. to cover the seed bed with a network of black cotton attached to twigs. Even this, however, is not entirely satisfactory, particularly if kittens are around. They have a habit of treating the cotton as though it were a maze specially designed for their own amusement. After a long experience of cats and gardens I have decided that the wisest and cheapest thing to do is to forget about seeds and buy boxes of seedlings.

There should be no need, one hopes, to remind the experienced F of the dangers which may lie waiting for cats in gardens where such things as weed killers are used. And yet, when I think of my own shortcomings in this respect, I feel that a word of warning would not be out of place.

Never, as long as I live, will I forget the awful drama of 'One', the Scotch firs, and the nicotine powder. I had planted a coppice of Scotch firs, at the end of the orchard at Merry Hall. If you have never planted Scotch firs you might be pardoned for thinking that they were a fairly simple tree to grow. They are not. They always develop — at least, mine do — a horrible little bug at the tip of the new growth, which burrows into the tender skin and eventually kills it. This means the loss of a year's growth.

What to do? At first, I used to go round every tree, search out the bugs, and gouge them to death by impaling them with sharp end of a twig. This was (a) exhausting and (b) stomach-turning, because the bugs, when gouged, turned into a peculiarly repellent form of yellow custard. Then I began to experiment with various sprays, none of which had the least effect. At last, I discovered nicotine powder. One applied it by means of a thing that looked like an attenuated concertina, which produced clouds of acrid dust, when shaken. This completely devastated the bugs, and the pine trees shot up, straight and green and immaculate.

But I had not realized that nicotine powder was a deadly poison and in the second year I was filled with feelings of such loathing for the bugs — who had started all over again — that I used it in quite inordinate quantities, so that a lot of it spattered the grass below. And that was how 'One' picked it up, and sampled it with his pink tongue, and felt the pangs of death inside him. Never shall I forget seeing him staggering towards me across the lawn, his eyes glazed, his body twisted with pain. This is a beastly memory, and I won't dwell on the twenty-four hours which ensued, where 'One' lay moaning in a dark cupboard. The only reason why I recall the episode is to remind Fs, if ever they should have recourse to poison, to use it with the utmost discretion. Better still, not to use it at all.

Apart from this one exception, all my memories of cats and gardens are ringed with happiness. At random I recall the blue of 'One's' eyes reflecting the blue of the tall clusters of anchusas under which he used to dispose himself on hot summer afternoons. I would wander out to the herbaceous border — probably for the twentieth time during the day — and see the anchusas looking faintly disturbed, and step softly over the parched earth, and find him there in the cool green shade that was starred with the miraculous blue of the flowers. I would speak to him, and the sleepy eyes would open, and two blues would melt together … and I would feel that this was one of those moments of peace and beauty which made up for all the struggles and heartaches of life.

H stands for History.

This letter should really be dedicated to Christabel[1] for without her classic *Dictionary of Cat-Lovers* it could not have been compiled. Never was there a wiser, more seductive anthology, in which the erudition is worn as lightly as a feather drifting past the wondering eyes of a kitten. It seems difficult to believe that the inspiration for this work, which is curiously feminine in spite of the weight of its scholarship, came at one of the most sombre moments of the war, in a darkened train, while an 'Alert' was sounding. A fellow passenger observed that the sound of the sirens was 'like the screaming of demon cats in agony'. This unknown traveller proved, in subsequent conversation, to be F. Sitting next to him was a militant non-F. The other occupants of the carriage were F and semi-F. They talked, they argued, the train rattled on through the mysterious blackness of the countryside; Christabel sat in a corner and thought her thoughts. And that was how it all began.

With a few of the facts in this dictionary I was already familiar; whenever I have been reading history, the appearance of a cat on the stage, even for a fleeting moment, has been enough to fix the event in my memory for ever. (I have often regretted that cats played no part in the interminable religious squabbles of the sixteenth century; a few brisk tabbies, waltzing through the Thirty-Nine Articles, might have given those arid paragraphs a semblance of interest.) And cats *have* made a great many appearances on the world's stage, often in the most distinguished company. One of the most persistent legends of the East concerns the prophet Mahomet who so greatly loved his cat that once, when it was

---

[1] The Dowager Lady Aberconway.

44

sleeping by his side, he cut off the sleeve of his robe rather than disturb it. Here indeed was a master F, and one could only wish that the modern inhabitants of the Arab countries, who are not noticeably kind to animals, had taken his lesson to heart.

All the true Fs at some time or other have emulated Mahomet's example ... not perhaps so drastically as to cut off portions of their attire, but enough to put themselves to considerable inconvenience. Such a one was President Theodore Roosevelt, whose term of office, though marked by other events of minor importance, was particularly memorable because of the role played by Slippers, the White House Cat. Slippers was grey, and he had six toes on each foot which earned him his curious name. My favourite story about him concerns a very grand diplomatic dinner party where he lay on his back in the middle of a narrow corridor down which the President and his guests had to make their way. It was a glittering procession of ambassadors and ambassadresses, but Slippers quite rightly took precedence over all of them. Rather than disturb him the President bowed low, and steered his ambassadress to one side. (She was not amused, for she was noticeably non-F.) 'Whereupon', writes the chronicler, 'the representatives of Great Britain and of France, of Germany and Italy, of all the empires and of the little kingdoms, followed suit, paying their respects to Slippers quite as effectually as if the warships of their nations had thundered out a salute.' Which, of course, is how it should be.

The above story has been quoted fairly frequently, but there is

one — even more remarkable because it concerns George Washington — which I have never seen in print. Apparently Washington was so eminently F that at Mount Vernon he actually made a cat-door for his own cat with his own hands — an ingenious little contrivance leading from the study to the garden. Moreover, this door can be seen by tourists to this day. This, surely, is the most important news; it is also yet another example of the strange obtuseness of the historians. For though I have been conducted more than once round Mount Vernon, and been regaled at length with quantities of details about Washington's career, nobody ever dreamt of pointing to the most important relic in the house ... the cat-door. Nor, as far as I can recall, have any historians mentioned that Washington was F at all. They prefer to inform us that he never told a lie — an omission which, one would have thought, it would have been kinder to hush up.

Quite evidently, the creation of cat-doors is the mark of a noble mind, and a lofty spirit of independence which cherishes freedom not only for man but for beast. One of the most illustrious cat-doors recorded in history was cut by the great Isaac Newton; indeed, he cut two of them, one large hole for his cat, and one small hole for her kitten. This fact might be borne in mind by Fs who occasionally engage in arguments with non-Fs.

I suggested above that even the Thirty-Nine Articles might have been enlivened by a little feline diversion. This did in fact once occur, in the House of Commons, or something very like it. In July of the year 1874 there was a debate on the Public Worship Regulation Bill. It was a boring subject, expounded by a very boring man, Sir William Harcourt, in the presence of the supreme bore of all time, Mr Gladstone. Suddenly an immense grey tabby cat stalked grandly down the opposition gangway, turned its head, took one look at Sir William Harcourt, registered disgust ... Harcourt was obviously non-F ... and shot out of the House, over the shoulders of the members sitting on the front Ministerial bench.

Perhaps it is because of their own fierce love of freedom that cats have always shown a strange sympathy for prisoners. One of these was Henry Wriothesly, third Earl of Southampton, the friend of Shakespeare and one of the posthumous contestants for the role of 'onlie begetter' of the sonnets. Well, he seems as likely a candidate as any of the others, particularly after one has studied the portrait of him at Welbeck. This shows a young man with wide, dreaming eyes, pale delicate hands, and in the background a most beguiling cat, glossy and relaxed and evidently well tended. When Southampton married, he incurred the disfavour of Elizabeth — who was, of course, blatantly non-F. He was sentenced to solitary confinement for life, in the Tower. This was too much for his favourite cat, who found its way to the Tower and climbed down the chimney into his apartment where, so the legend goes, it stayed with him to the end. This is one of the pleasantest examples of the fact that a cat can not only look at a Queen, but flout her authority.

But the most celebrated case of a cat who cared for a prisoner is afforded by Sir Henry Wyatt in the fifteenth century. Because of his loyalty to the Lancastrian party, Richard III threw him in one of his foulest prisons 'where hee had neither bed to lie on, nor cloaths sufficient to warme him, nor meate for his mouth'. And while he lay there in these dreadful circumstances, a cat — realizing that a true F was in great distress — made her way into the dungeon and offered her services. 'And after this, shee would come every day unto him, divers times, and when shee could gett one, bring him a pigeon.'

This pigeon, to the non-F, may sound like a 'property' bird. But the legend, not only to the F but to the historian, has the ring of truth, and it is reinforced by a strangely moving contemporary portrait of Wyatt, in his later years, sitting in prison beside his cat, who is gazing at him in adoration and at the same time somewhat incongruously manipulating a pigeon through the bars of the cell.

I have indicated, very briefly, a few of the roles which cats have played in history. Lest I should be accused of undue partiality, let us end with the story of the Empress Wu. (It is conceivable that some people may have forgotten that the Empress Wu was the protégé of the Empress Wang, whom she eventually supplanted in the year 683. However, every schoolboy knows that the Empress Wang ... or was it Wong? ... was hostile to the concubine Hsiao who was the favourite of the Emperor T'ai Tsung. One almost blushes to remind the reader that Wu married the Emperor Kao Tsung. Anyway, to cut a long story short, in more senses than one, Wu eventually chopped off everybody's hands and feet, Wang's, Wong's, T'ai Tsung's, Kao Tsung's and Uncle Tom Cobley's and all.)

Wu was unabashedly F. One says this with a certain diffidence, for she would seem, at this distance, to have had a strain of ruthlessness in her character. And yet, how are we to know whether Wang — or Wong — and T'ai Tsung and Kao Tsung were not even more ruthless? Be that as it may, Wu had some very modern ideas. She was extremely worried about the warring sects of her empire, and she was anxious to unite them in one great peaceful federation. So she decided to set them an example. With the assistance of her official censor P'eng-Hsien-Chueh (that will be the last one) she trained her cat, whose name is fortunately lost in the mists of time, to eat off the same plate as her parrot. A great Exhibition was staged, to show this amiable phenomenon to the warring chieftains. Unfortunately something went wrong; the anonymous pussy was hungry. So it bit off the parrot's head and ate it.

History records that the Empress was 'very much embarrassed'. One's own reaction is that even cats, in off moments, will behave very much like members of the United Nations.

I stands for Inventions.

I have always regretted that cats cannot be provided with latch-keys. However domesticated they may appear to be, they are wild creatures at heart, and as the darkness falls they hear the call of the jungle. True, the jungle may be only a backyard, and the tropical undergrowth may be confined to a speckled laurel and a cluster of bedraggled ivy. But at least it is in the open air, under the stars, and the night wind is tingling with a thousand mysterious scents. And the wall can be leapt upon, and stalked along, and transformed into a magic thoroughfare.

To keep a cat indoors, night after night, with nothing to do but to stare at this dark paradise through a pane of glass, and lash its tail impotently against the net curtains, seems to me grossly inconsiderate, if not actually cruel. If I myself had been a cat in the days of the Regency — and I have sober reasons for believing this to have been the case -- I should have described it as 'the outside of enough'.

Hence my invention of the cat-door. I call it 'my' invention, for though Newton, as we have seen, thought of it first, I thought of it long before I knew that Newton had thought about it. However, no true F would wish to claim exclusive rights in so beneficent an invention, still less to patent it. On the contrary, I would like to see more and more cat-doors, bigger and better cat-doors, appearing all over the country. I would like the electorate to become cat-door-conscious, and if I were on the London County Council I would vote for cat-doors to be made compulsory on all new building estates, with a high priority over such inessentials as damp-courses and fire escapes.

The making of a cat-door can be very simply described. All you have to do is to cut out a square of wood near the base of one of the doors in your house. Most people will probably choose the door of the kitchen. Then you cut an inch off the bottom of the square of wood and refix by means of a pair of pivots. It will then swing backwards and forwards quite easily.

I should perhaps warn you that in spite of the naked simplicity of this device, the average carpenter will approach it with mistrust, indeed with trepidation. There will be a great deal of argument about it. But eventually, if he perseveres, the true F will wear the carpenter down.

I have two cat-doors in my own house; one of them leads from the kitchen down a flight of steps into a little courtyard; the other leads straight from the music-room on to the open lawn. The gentle sound of the doors swinging backwards and forwards at all times of the day and the night, is a pleasing accompaniment to my life; it reminds me that the cats are alert and fully occupied and intent upon their many tasks of inspection, espionage and sentry work. Often, when I have been feeling lonely, when a book has been thrust aside in boredom, when the keys of the piano, softly lit, hold no invitation to the dance, I have lain back and stared at the shadows on the ceiling, wondering what life is all about ... and then, suddenly, there is the echo of the swinging door, and across the carpet, walking with the utmost delicacy and precision, stalks 'Four' or 'Five' or Oscar. Whichever it may be, his tail is always very upright, and as he walks he talks ... small, friendly, feline talk, delivered in the softest of mews ... mews which melt into purrs as he approaches the sofa. He sits down on the floor beside me, regarding my long legs, my old jumper, and my floppy arms, with a purely practical interest. Which part of this large male body will form the most appropriate lap? Usually he settles for the chest. Whereupon he springs up and there is a feeling of cold fur — for the night is frosty — and the tip of an icy nose, thrust against my wrist and a positive tattoo of purrs. And I no longer wonder what life is all about.

Some very spoiled cats, after a while, develop a habit of sitting in front of the cat-door with an air of profound pathos, pretending that they do not understand how to get through it. They peer through the little gap at the bottom, they heave profound sighs, they gaze up with anguished expressions, pleading that the door may be opened for them in the ordinary way.

When this happens, the owner must be ruthless. He must steel his heart. The cat knows perfectly well how to go through the cat-door; it has gone through at least a thousand times; and this sudden reluctance to use it is simply an 'act'. It is merely doing it to annoy, because it knows it teases. The owner must not allow himself to be blackmailed in this manner. In no circumstances must he open the door. His best plan is to be quite nonchalant. A little light-hearted conversation about the weather ... a swift, delicate stroke ... a few bars, hummed quite casually, of a popular tune. He must not allow the atmosphere to grow too tense. Otherwise he will gradually be hypnotized by those appealing eyes, and he will find himself opening the door, willy-nilly.

With kittens, on their first introduction to the door, his technique will of course be very different. He should first swing the door gently backwards and forwards in order to make the kitten familiar with its movement. Then, for a few moments, he should hold the door open, extended outwards, so that the kitten may be assured that there is nothing sinister on the other side. After which he should lift the kitten with great firmness, press its paws against the door, and push it through. This action may possibly be resented by the kitten, who will dart away under the nearest rhododendron, and refuse to be coaxed inside until it has caused the maximum of trouble. But little by little the kitten will accustom itself to the door, and use it as a matter of course.

To sum up, Fs who have not equipped themselves with cat-doors should give the matter their early and earnest consideration. True, they may be meticulous about leaving the kitchen window open. They may have evolved the most elaborate technique about letting pussy out at night, and tapping plates with a fork to get her back again. But these are merely makeshifts. Without a cat-door the owner of a house is living, from an F point of view, in the Middle Ages.

J stands for Journeys.

At some time or other of their lives nearly all Fs — and quite a large number of non-Fs — have had the scarifying experience of transporting pussy, by car or by rail, to a new home. The word 'scarifying' is bracketed in Roget's *Thesaurus* with such words as 'crushing', 'harrowing', 'torturing', 'agonizing' and 'cruciating'. There are also cross-references to 'daggers in the breast' and 'thorns in the side'. For the purposes of this section of our alphabet all these expressions are strictly apposite.

Perhaps the most 'scarifying' — or, to revert to Roget, 'pothering', 'corroding' and altogether 'wherreting' — experience I ever had of cat transport was during the war, when I was obliged to drive no less than five Siamese cats to a safe area all the way from London to Devonshire. It had to be done on the spur of the moment, after a night of fire-watching, through smoking streets that were railed off with the sinister sign 'Unexploded Bomb'. As I drove, the wail of the sirens blended in a sort of infernal harmony with the wail of the Siamese cats, who were struggling in baskets which were far too small for them. I was alone, I had no time to stop and comfort them, and by the journey's end I was even nearer to nervous collapse than the cats themselves. And though I love the wail of a Siamese, there are times when, for a fleeting second, it still strikes a chill to my heart.

Happily, most of the journeys we take with cats are less wherreting. However, they are quite wherreting enough. Here, therefore, are a few hints which — though they will seem trite to the expert Fs — may perhaps be of value to less experienced persons.

Let us assume that only one pussy is to be transported — a simple, uncomplicated pussy of some three summers — and that the journey involves a short trip by motor car and a longer trip by train. The first question to be answered is ... what shall we carry her in? By far the most satisfactory conveyance, in my experience, is a linen basket, which allows plenty of air, and enough, but not too much, light. The basket should of course be lined with something soft, ideally a rug or a blanket on which pussy has been accustomed to sleep.

We will draw a veil over the painful process of putting pussy into the basket, lifting her into the car, and carrying her through the frightening racket of the station. There are no particular technical difficulties involved in these procedures, all that is needed is a kind heart, a sound stomach, nerves of steel, and a hide of brass ... the latter in order to enable one to face the outraged looks of one's travelling companions, who invariably assume, from the piercing wails that come from the basket, that one is some exceptionally degraded type of cat-torturer.

Now comes a point of exceptional importance.

Whatever else you may do, never let pussy out of the basket.

The wails may rise to agonizing heights, they may be charged with bitter reproach and desperate entreaty, but you must harden your heart. This is one of those occasions when you really must 'be cruel to be kind'. (That is a phrase I have never greatly cared for; it has a nasty echo of 'spare the rod and spoil the child'. I suspect that there are occasions when the cruel-to-be-kind fraternity secretly enjoy the act of cruelty.)

But surely, this is an occasion when the phrase rings true. For which is the greater cruelty ... to keep pussy in the basket, or to let her out? In the basket, admittedly, she is cramped, but she is not actually in pain. She has plenty of air. She is not in the dark. And though the whole situation is strange and frightening, at least she has a familiar voice to comfort her, and a familiar finger to scratch her head.

But if she is let out she immediately leaps into a world of sheer terror, a world of blinding lights and darting shadows, speeding by at sixty miles per hour. She can have only one impulse in her wildly beating heart, to escape ... anyhow, anywhere, at any cost, back to the quiet

world from which you have so recently dragged her. And escape, unless you are very careful, she will. A cat in these circumstances is endowed with the strength of a fiend, and even a small Siamese kitten is a full-time job.

We have observed, time and again, that this is intended to be a sternly practical book. A book in which the prose gives pride of place to the precept. A book destined for the dusty shelves of veterinary surgeons, where it will stand next to such volumes as *Cows — their Cause and Cure*. Why it should so often be necessary to remind myself of this patent fact I find it hard to say; perhaps it is because 'Five' has been so constantly perched on the desk beside me, giving a playful dab to my pen.

Whatever the reason, we will now substantiate our claim.

For this is where we invoke the aid of science, in the shape of a mild, soothing pill, with 'Four', 'Five' and Oscar as examples of its efficacy.

Before doing so, however, it is only fair to point out that 'Four', 'Five' and Oscar may perhaps be regarded as somewhat exceptional felines. They have enjoyed a superior education. They have a wide and cosmopolitan circle of human acquaintances. Moreover, they have been accustomed to publicity. They have not sought it, but it has been thrust upon them. They are fully accustomed to being lifted from repose and seated upon chairs in the music-room in order to pose for young gentlemen

who stand before them and flash bulbs at them. True, they seldom pose for long. Indeed, one flash is usually enough to send them scurrying out through the cat-door into the garden, from which I refuse to rescue them, because I do not wish them to be subjected to too much nervous strain. All the same, I believe they rather like publicity, in their secret hearts. Every Christmas I prepare a little cat calendar which has a modest sale in the F world. This has a photograph of a cat for every month, with a few words from myself underneath each photograph. Nearly always I manage to squeeze in a picture of 'Four', 'Five' and Oscar. But last year 'Five' had to be left out, and was supplanted by a Siamese kitten, of exceptional allurement, dabbing at a spray of pear-blossom. When the calendar was placed on Gaskin's mantelpiece, a few days before Christmas, 'Five' took one look at it, registered acute disgust, and stalked out into the garden in a fit of sulks.

Back to science and the soothing pill. 'Surely,' the reader may ask, 'there can be no need of soporifics with cats who are so used to the bright lights? Surely they would face the sternest of ordeals with equanimity, and display their habitual sang-froid even if they were obliged to ride through London in the Lord Mayor's coach?' This is not the case. My cats, when they feel like it, can be as temperamental as anybody else's. Every Tuesday morning, for instance, at approximately ten o'clock, the whole household is disorganized by cats shooting violently in all directions, in a state of the greatest alarm. Oscar rushes to a cupboard, 'Five' leaps on to a tallboy, 'Four' squeezes under Gaskin's bed. The cause of all this commotion is an agreeable young dustman, going his weekly round. All he has done is to bang the lids of the dustbins. Moreover — as I have gathered from casual conversation — he is a highly civilized person, who spends his dustman's money on long playing records of Khatchaturyian. (Which may account for the vigour with which he percusses the lids.) In spite of this, as far as 'Four', 'Five' and Oscar are concerned, he might be a fiend incarnate, clanging them to hell.

I repeat, my cats are just as temperamental as yours. And yet, a single little pill enabled them to make the journey from Merry Hall to Richmond with complete tranquillity. They were not transported, they were wafted. They yawned, they disposed themselves in the baskets, they

curled themselves up, and if they had been confined to the use of the English language, they would have murmured ... 'Home Charles, and avoid the Kingston by-pass.'

I do not know the name of the pill. But any good vet., surely, will know about it, and be able to instruct you in its use. It does not actually send pussy to sleep, and it does not entirely prevent an occasional faint mew of protest from the inside of the basket. But it is a mew that ends in a yawn, and the yawning seems to persist, in lessening degrees, for about forty-eight hours. By when, let us hope, pussy will be firmly re-established and her new life will have begun.

K stands for Kneading.

This refers, of course, to the charming alternating movement of the front paws made by pussy in moments of great contentment. First one paw is raised and then the other, with the utmost grace; the claws are slightly but amiably protruded; sometimes the eyes are narrowed. This is evidently an hour when all is right with the world.

I have sometimes thought that this delightful accomplishment might be renamed 'Organ-Playing'. This demands a word of explanation. Occasionally, in order to enter more closely into the minds of cats, I have endeavoured to copy their physical habits. I am past the age for rushing up the trunks of apple trees or for skidding down them. ('Skidding' is, I think, the right word with which to describe the action of a cat descending the trunk of a tree. They never seem quite happy about it. I am sure that all Fs will have shared with me those moments of agonized apprehension when one has stood at the foot of a tall tree ... usually at dusk in a high wind ... trying to coax some foolhardy creature back to earth. This is one of the few occasions when cats seem to lose their heads. Below them stretches the nice broad, solid trunk of the tree, waiting to conduct them to safety. At the bottom of the trunk stands their master, making the most ingratiating noises, and — in cases of extremity — tapping a plate of fish. But they pay no heed. Just when one thinks that they are near enough to be reached by a ladder, off they dart down some truant branch, and sway and stagger and balance in the wind, making the most piteous noises.)

But all this is taking us away from the matter under discussion — organ-playing. As I was saying, there are days when I try to enter into the feline mind by emulating their physical habits. It was my cat 'Five' who gave me my first organ lesson, one day when I was lying in bed. Until that morning I had always regarded this movement as 'kneading'. 'Five' was looking at me with a very intent expression, as though he were challenging me to a kneading competition. 'Very well,' I said to him, 'if you desire me to knead, I will knead. It will be a useful Yogi exercise in tranquillity and spiritual elevation.' So I pushed aside an extremely brutal issue of *Life*, filled with photographs of corpses stretched on beaches in Malaya, and began ... tentatively ... to 'knead'. I say 'tentatively' because an amateur is always embarrassed in the presence of a professional. And then, all of a sudden, I forgot 'Five' and his green, appraising eyes, for I realized that I was inadvertently playing the slow movement of Bach's Italian Concerto on the blanket. The melody, slightly muffled in wool, was unmistakable, the bass — faintly entangled in the sheets — was adequate. As I continued to 'knead' I found myself pulling out invisible stops — here a vox humana, there a cor anglais or a tremolo.

Try it for yourself, and you will see what I mean.

All my three cats are expert organists, but their techniques vary greatly and their repertoires are quite different. 'Five' specializes in quiet chorales, 'Four' in Bach fugues. The most spectacular player is Oscar, whose favourite composer is evidently Mahler. When Oscar leaps on to my bed, to give a recital, his paws pound the blankets — which are of the cellular variety — with such frenzy that small skeins of wool are detached. A tremendous bass purr echoes from the depths of his white chest, and the eyes are half closed in ecstasy. It is a moving and impressive performance, which has only one drawback. So exalted does Oscar become that he is inclined to dribble. A simple solution to this problem will be found in the chapter devoted to Purring.

There is an infinite variety of techniques in feline organ-playing. To me, one of the most charming is when pussy is sitting at one's feet, and gazing up at one, and — because her mood is amiable and the sun is shining — she very lightly touches the keys, as it were, with one paw. Only Fs will realize that she is playing the organ at all, for this is indeed the most subtle and elusive form of feline music.

Pussy may sometimes decide to play the organ in circumstances inconvenient to her master, for example, on his knees. This frequently occurs during the watching of television. Pussy, observing a lap — for even gentlemen, if properly trained, are capable of forming laps — will spring up, curl around, face the screen, purr, and begin to run her paws lightly over the keyboard, in other words, to dig her claws into the owner's knees.

This is a moment when all Fs have an opportunity of proving their quality. Non-Fs, needless to say, will immediately push pussy off their laps with some crude and vulgar expletive, and if they are of an exceptionally beastly disposition, they will give pussy a slap.

But the true F will grin and bear it. If the organ-playing becomes particularly passionate he can comfort himself with the thought that there is probably some iodine in the bathroom.

L stands for going to the Loo.

This section might also have come under P for Powdering the Nose, or W for Washing the Hands. It should be skipped by persons of excessive sensibility.

To all true Fs the feline routine of going to the Loo, particularly if the Loo is situated in a large garden, and not too near the seedlings, is an elegant and entirely inoffensive performance ... which is more than can be said for similar operations by members of the human race.

It is also, for me at any rate, a mysterious and somewhat awe-inspiring spectacle. From what distant ages were those intricate techniques handed down? From what ancient volume of etiquette has the smallest kitten learned how to behave, as it totters on to its box of sand and gives its first feeble scrape with the left

paw? (Kittens always start with the *left* paw ... a fact which I should have brought to the attention of Mr Darwin if I had been honoured with his friendship. In later life they use either paw indiscriminately.)

The whole thing is as formal and as stately as a minuet. Pussy walks across the lawn, to go to the Loo. Which, of the myriad loos at her disposal, shall she choose? The seedling bed, needless to say, would be ideal, but she recalls that the last time she used it there was a most ridiculous commotion. Perhaps it had better be the kitchen garden, where humans are not so fussy. So off she goes, and finds a very pleasing loo in the shape of a patch of newly dug earth. Out comes her paw ... and then, unaccountably, she changes her mind. A superior loo, about ten feet away, has suggested itself. But no ... the first one was better. So back she goes. One paw comes out again, and scrapes and scrapes (always one paw at a time) ... and then the other, till all is in readiness. And then, the act. Very still, head erect, shoulders back. Like a statue from the era of Tutankhamen. A wild creature, performing an essential function, with the utmost dignity and distinction.

The post-operative technique, to use a piece of jargon from the surgical ward, is not without its interest. In the interests of feline hygiene there must be more scraping, to conceal any displeasing evidence of what has occurred. But the scraping seems to go to pussy's head. Even after the hygienic necessities have been observed there will be more scrapings, apparently at random, first with one paw, then with the other paw, with the sweet earth shooting out in all directions.

Indeed, it would seem that the very act of going to the loo, or rather, of having gone to the loo, produces in pussy a feeling of inexplicable exhilaration. Consider one of my own cats, 'Four', whose favourite loo is situated on the rhododendron bank. As soon as the last delicate sweep has scattered the last fragment of earth, there is a dramatic pause, in which he stares around him in wild surmise. And then, suddenly, he shoots across the lawn towards the house at lightning speed, bound upon bound, whiskers flying in the wind, tail as erect as a pennant ... a streamlined symbol of delight.

I have often thought how interesting it would be if this conduct were general among human beings. Suppose that one were walking down the corridor of a French hotel, past the door marked 'Dames'. Suppose that the door were suddenly to be flung open, revealing a lady who stood in the entrance, clasping her hands and gazing around her with starry eyes and parted lips. And suppose that she were then to break into peals of girlish laughter and rush down the corridor, screaming 'Je sors de la toilette, je sors de la toilette délicieuse!' One would be enthralled. This is yet another example of the fact that females have much to learn from felines.

In an emergency, pussy will go to the utmost trouble in order to keep up her high standard of cleanliness. Normally, of course, if she wishes to 'leave the room', she walks with calm dignity to the door, looks over her shoulder, and waits for the door to be opened. But if she is shut up alone in a house where there is no means of exit, without even a box for her convenience, and if she is unable to wait any longer, she usually seeks high and low for some place where she will cause the minimum of inconvenience. Once, years ago, when I had a tiny house in Westminster, I gave shelter to a thin, battered alley cat whom I had found drenched with rain, crouched forlornly in the gardens outside the Houses of Parliament. For a little while, all was well, and life flowed by smoothly enough, with pussy settling down, consuming large quantities of fish, and showing no desire to go out except for occasional sorties to the large variety of feline toilettes that were available in the surrounding backyards. Then one night, I was delayed in the country, and pussy was shut up all alone for twenty-four hours. I returned in some apprehension ... not because I was worried by any possible damage to carpets but because I hated to think that I had been the unwitting cause of embarrassment or even pain to a creature who had honoured me with its friendship.

I opened the door and called. No pussy. I walked into the little kitchen. The fish plate was wiped clean, even of the bones, the saucer of milk was empty ... but that could soon be remedied. I hurried up the stairs, still calling, and as I reached the top step I saw pussy emerging from the bathroom. I took her in my arms, and there was a soft purring, but I seemed to hear in the purring a faint echo of apprehension, as though she were not quite certain of her welcome. I set her down; in a moment I would see to the fish and open the back window, but first I must wash my hands. I stepped into the bathroom, and as I did so, I saw that pussy had had the same idea; she too had washed her hands, with as much delicacy as was possible in the circumstances, precisely over the plug in the bath.

We do well to remember that cats are creatures of the jungle, that their eyes are lit with forest fires. But equally we should remember that they carry in their minds this strange understanding of some of the essentials of civilization, as though in some remote far-shadowed past they had dwelled in cities of their own building.

M stands for Mew.
Mews may be divided into three classes:

1. The sad mew
2. The conversational mew
3. The utilitarian mew.

There are several sub-divisions of these main categories. We will deal with them in due course.

1. Concerning the sad mew, we will not write, for these are meant to be happy pages, where we can, at least for a while, forget the sorrows of the world. All the fears and bewilderments of the little helpless creatures of the animal kingdom are reflected in the mew of a kitten that is lost. In real life we would not pass on, but here, we may.

2. The conversational mew is heard to its best advantage on a summer evening, when the cat is at the far end of the lawn and suddenly sees his master approaching. Whereupon the cat turns and begins to walk towards his master. As he walks, he talks. Needless to say, there are many pauses in this progress, for there are patches of grass to be sniffed, and fallen leaves to be inspected; but as soon as these duties are performed, the promenade is resumed ... always to the accompaniment of conversation. This is a sort of feline small talk; if it were translated it would probably be found to consist in comments on the weather, the extraordinary behaviour of the hedgehog under the copper beech, and the callousness of the gardener, whose weed-killer stings the paws. To which one would

retort that it is better for pussy's paws to tingle for a few minutes than for pussy to be poisoned.

3. The utilitarian mew is most commonly heard outside closed doors. Even, I regret to say, outside some of the doors in my own house. For though there is a cat-door from the garden into my kitchen, and another cat-door from the kitchen into the dining-room, one cannot have cat-doors in every room.

Mews outside doors, it need hardly be said, should be instantly obeyed by cat-owners. How would the average human feel if every time he wished to leave the room he was obliged to sit on a mat and mew? However, lest it be assumed that we are carrying courtesy to extremes, we will admit that there are moments when, having opened a door for pussy, we have wished pussy would make up her mind as to whether she wants to go in or out. Only too often pussy remains poised half way, tail twitching, staring down the corridor, so that one cannot shut the door without endangering the tail. I have never been able to make up my mind whether it is permissible on such occasions to give pussy a slight prod. I admit that I have sometimes done this, but always at the cost of remorse.

Now for some of the variations on the three main classes of mew, which should be familiar to all serious students.

A. The purr-mew. This is one of the gentlest and most soothing sounds in a predominantly discordant world; it is the music made by a mother-cat to its kittens, particularly when her master leans over the

basket and strokes one of the kittens on its small, warm, square head. Then the purr-mew is heard at its best ... a strange, treble trilling that breaks into a single note.

B. The almost silent mew. This is extremely subtle, and associated with moments of complete well-being and comfort. It is the faint sound that comes from a happy, sleepy cat, stretched out in front of a fire, when its master gently disturbs its dreams. One eyelid flickers, disclosing a line of liquid green, the mouth is very slightly opened, and then pianissimo comes this tiny sound, so faint that it is scarcely heard. After which the eyelid flickers back, the mouth is closed, and there is silence again. And the owner, if he has been properly brought up, tiptoes from the room.

C. The Siamese mew. This should perhaps be put in a class of its own, for it has a quite special timbre, and an exquisite resonance which must surely be the envy of all other felines. One has heard that there are some afflicted persons who are deaf to the beauty of the Siamese mew; such people, if they indeed exist, are deeply to be pitied. Should we ever encounter them we must be especially considerate to them, always remembering how much life has denied to them.[1] For the wild music of the Siamese mew is something without which no life can be considered quite complete. There is no true parallel to it, either in the world of nature or of art, and the only creatures who seem sometimes to echo this strange, bittersweet call are the gulls, wheeling inland when the wind is high.

---

[1] The mew is an infallible touchstone in exposing non-Fs who pose as Fs. Sometimes one is visited by people who, desiring to create a good impression, pretend to be fond of cats. When one's cat enters the room, these persons force a smile on their faces, and emit a hideous sound which is spelt MIAOW, thinking to ingratiate themselves (*a*) with the cat, and (*b*) with its master. Needless to say, the cat stares at them with horror and beats a hasty retreat. The owner, unfortunately, cannot follow its example. But at least he can be thankful that the non-F has revealed himself in his true colours, and if he has any sense he will take the first opportunity of locking up the silver.

N stands for Names.

The first of my cats of whom there is any historical record was a black kitten called Pasht. He appears on the third page of a novel called *Prelude*, which I wrote at the age of seventeen. I have just taken down a faded copy from my shelves to refresh my memory about him. Pasht plays a small but important role in the story. He was the last and most precious object to whom my hero, Paul — who was of course myself — said goodbye before leaving for his first day at the public school of Marlborough.

Paul wandered slowly round the room saying goodbye to all the little things he loved. Suddenly he noticed a small black lump on the bed. It turned out to be Pasht, his kitten. It looked up at him with sleepy eyes, and put out a limp paw. Paul closed his eyes and rubbed his face in its short black fur. How cold its tiny nose was against his forehead! Oh God, how awful to have to say goodbye to this true faithful Pasht that he had loved for at least six weeks! He put him down and stared at the bed. Would he have a bed at Marlborough? He supposed they did have them there, but was by no means sure about it.

If I were in the habit of smiling wistfully, I should certainly do so after reading those lines. I may not have been a very nice boy — there must surely be something wrong about seventeen-year-old novelists — but I seem to have had redeeming qualities.

The choice of Pasht as the name for a kitten suggests a certain schoolboy precocity, particularly when I remember that he was joined a year later by another black kitten whom I called Baudelaire. I had been caned, at school, for reading *Les Fleurs du Mal* in class. Admittedly, this may not be ideal literature for schoolboys, but there was so much fresh air at Marlborough, so many cold baths, so much hearty hymn-singing and so many small boys running about in shorts, obviously destined to be low church bishops, that a small dose of decadent and heavily perfumed French poetry might have been regarded as a healthy corrective. I suggested as much to my form master, who gave me ten strokes as a consequence. This treatment only enhanced my regard for the poet, and I sat down rather gingerly to learn by heart his sensuous poem 'Le Chat'. Some readers may recall its first, haunting lines:

> Viens, mon beau chat, sur mon cœur amoureux
> Retiens les griffes de ta patte,
> Et laisse-moi plonger dans tes beaux yeux
> Mêlés de métal et d'agate.

Pasht and Baudelaire have long since passed on, though I hope that one day I may encounter them again. I cannot imagine a heaven without animals. (I find no sort of difficulty, on the other hand, in imagining a heaven without humans!) And whenever I conjure up a vision of the Pearly Gates, I find that black kittens always seem to find a place in it. They dart about making dabs at St Peter's robes, and very glossy and shiny their fur looks against the columns of the Gates, which, in my version, are made of extremely expensive mother-of-pearl.

But we were talking about names.

Have you noticed that other people's names for their cats are so often inapposite? For instance, one is introduced to an exceptionally refined creature with grey fur and topaz eyes, a cat who should spend a large part of its life gazing amiably on to a cathedral close, supervising the goings-on of the rural dean — and one is told that its name is Whiskey. How anybody can possibly attach the name of such a fluid to so delicious an object as a cat is beyond comprehension. Some cats, indeed, are given names which have a suspicion of actual contempt such as Smuts or Spotty. The true F, surely, should know better than this. Such names may be good enough for children, they are certainly not good enough for cats.

If history were properly taught at school — by which I mean that if cats and queens were treated with equal respect — there would be fewer examples of this unfortunate tendency. The pages of the past are richly · studded with enchanting names given to their pets by illustrious Fs. One recalls the fourteen cats of Cardinal Richelieu, of which the prettiest — nominally — were Felimare, Soumise, Mimie Paillou and Perruque. Then there was Carlyle's Columbine — which needless to say was detested by Mrs Carlyle, who was as non-F as her husband was F. Dr Erasmus Darwin's cat was called Persian Snow, and Dickens's cat was called — not by him but by the family — Williamina. The mystic Evelyn Underhill had a St Philip Neri, Lytton Strachey owned a Tiberius, and Sir Walter Scott chose the name Hinse of Hinsefield.

All these names show a proper respect for felinity, which is all too rare even in the best F circles.

After these remarks the reader may well inquire why, for the last fifteen years or so, I have chosen to call my cats by numbers. There are three reasons.

Firstly, because I write a great deal of fiction, which demands the invention of a host of names to fit the personalities of the characters.

Few readers realize how irksome this invention is, how fatiguing. A name must fit a character like a glove, and unless it is the right name the creature refuses to play. Imagine how quite impossible the whole story of David Copperfield would have seemed if the hero had swopped names with Uriah Heep. This is an extreme case; the flamboyant labels which were permissible in the days of Dickens would not be acceptable today. But though a writer can no longer permit himself the extravagance of a Mr Veneering or a Pecksniff, Miss Codger or Betsey Prigg, he must still conjure up in his mind a name which fits in colour, in musical tone, in a hundred subtle associations.

(As a matter of minor literary interest, I always have recourse to the A.B.C. railway guide, at least as far as the surnames are concerned. Many English family names have a territorial origin, and the pages of this admirable volume are rich in unexpected treasures.)

The second reason why I call my cats by numbers is because of recent years numbers have acquired a subtle elegance of their own. Perhaps this is due to the influence of that remarkable woman Madame Chanel and her Numero Cinq. This agreeable essence was originally the perquisite of a few rich ladies of French society, but after the war, when Paris was occupied by the forces of the United States, it ended up by perfuming the entire American Army. In spite of this, the faint atmosphere of elegance still clings round the number, and when I was adopted by my first Siamese kitten I decided to call him Number One.

A word about these numbers. 'Two' and 'Three' — both Siamese — were tragedies. They died when they were still kittens, victims of that dire scourge of the feline world, the cat flu. I would like to think that all

humans could put up so brave a fight for life as those two little kittens. After that, I swore that I would never have another Siamese — a vow that grows daily more difficult to keep.

Along came 'Four'. A kitten straight from the farm, black, perky, sentimental and altogether adorable. 'Four' has the best purr I have ever known, bar none, a purr with a quite astonishing vocal range. If he were not called 'Four' I should call him 'Callas', because his purr really has a prima donna quality. Moreover, it is still as sweet and flexible today as it was when he first jumped out of his basket. At the time of writing 'Four' is thirteen years old, which takes him, in human terms, well into the eighties. One wonders if the aforesaid diva will be purring quite so effectively at a similar age. One doubts it.

After 'Four' came 'Five', who is still very much with us, as you may have gathered.

'Six' presented us with a problem. He was an adorable shade of ginger, with spots on his nose, and paws as soft as a peach. But when he strayed too far into the orchard ... which he often did ... and when we followed him, calling 'Six ... Six ... Six ... ,' the result was, to say the least of it, inharmonious. If you will put down this volume for a moment, and say aloud the number six three times in rapid succession, you will see what I mean. So we decided that 'Six' should be omitted ... it should be The Cat Who Never Was, a mystic creature to tantalize our dreams. And 'Six' was rechristened 'Seven', and eventually — for this was a time of strife and turmoil — he was transported to the house of a very charming lady in Sussex, who had a kind heart and a large field and a number of old barns and outhouses in which he could prowl and hunt. Judging from the photographs which we sometimes receive of him, he has prowled and hunted to great effect.

Finally, came Oscar, who should have been 'Eight'. But he had already been christened, and as you may have gathered, he is a cat of such a vivid personality that any change of name would have been unthinkable.

Meanwhile, I lift a glass to 'Nine', 'Ten', 'Eleven' and 'Twelve', who are sleeping somewhere in the womb of Time. On the basis of the normal 'expectancy of life' — not only for myself but for my companions — 'Twelve' should be the last. I shall welcome him when he comes, but as yet I have no desire to meet him face to face.

O stands for Old Maids.

And O also stands, as far as I am concerned, for a protest against the callousness and stupidity of the non-F world.

One of the commoner sneers against the cat is the suggestion that it is the favourite pet of old maids. Why this — even if it it were true — should be regarded as a black mark against pussy, I am at a loss to understand. I have yet to learn that there is anything dishonourable either in old age or in solitude. And I consider it impertinence, indeed cruelty, to assume that because a woman has not married she has never had the chance to do so. There are countless reasons why a woman may not choose to marry, but if she is a true woman, she keeps them to herself. For which the world rewards her by sneering at her as an 'old maid'.

So if the cat does happen to be the favourite pet of the old maid, I think that this is a sign of excellent good sense of both parties. The life of an ageing, unmarried woman demands quiet friendship and gentle affection; it demands, above all, the companionship of a creature to whom home — the actual walls and windows and fireplaces and furnishings of home — are important and precious, apart from the human beings who inhabit them.

I often think that cats are 'house-proud'. Sometimes when I have paid a call at a house where a cat is in residence, I have felt a sharp eye fixed on me when I have been about to sit on a certain chair, as though pussy were saying: 'Kindly be careful with that chair; it's Hepplewhite and the legs are wonky.' And if the house happens to belong to one of the despised 'old maids' I feel that the cat is present in some subtle way in every part of the house and has, indeed, taken part in its arrangement. I can guess her favourite corners, can see how she would stretch out on the hearthrug, so close to the fire that you would think the fur of her tummy would be scorched, can picture her staring out of the window, and can even hear her, in imagination, making those extremely unrefined chattering noises at the birds.

An old house, old furniture, old pictures and ornaments, the faint scent of lavender in a bowl, and an old maid sitting by the fire with a cat on her lap ... what a perfect picture for the ridicule of the world! How deliciously amusing! Let's chuck a stone through her window!

But the old maid legend, of course, has no justification in fact. One does not usually associate the personnel of the British Navy with old maidishness, particularly the members of the lower deck, but sailors, ever since the Navy sailed the seas, have demanded that cats should come too, and have lavished on them quite remarkable affection even to the extent of risking their lives for them. The non-F may suggest that this is merely because the cat is a rat-catcher. To which the F has a ready retort. If the engineers who design such a streamlined monster as the modern aircraft carrier are unable to prevent their ships from being overrun by rats without invoking the superior technical abilities of pussy, they should hang their heads in shame.

This reminds me of a story narrated to me by the very gallant captain of a very glorious ship — the first *Ark Royal*, which led the Germans such a thrilling dance in the early days of the war. The *Ark Royal*

had its own feline contingent, consisting of a motley but exuberant collection of pussies collected by affectionate sailors, usually in somewhat alcoholic moments, from such places as Plymouth and Pompey. Whenever the ship came to a foreign port these pussies, it seems, were as anxious to go ashore as the sailors themselves; indeed, they insisted on their rights, and lined up with their tails erect and their whiskers bristling, as soon as the gangways were lowered. After all, if sailors could have a wife in every port, so could pussies. And husbands, too, it appeared, judging from several accouchements which took place after a courtesy visit to Naples.

But I was supposed to be telling a story. Here it is. Every time those pussies went ashore the captain of this great ship, who was of course impeccably F, heaved a sigh of regret and said to himself: 'Well, I suppose that we have said goodbye to them. I hope they fare well, but we shall never see them again.' A very reasonable assumption, as you will agree. For how could the pussies know when the ship was setting sail again? How could they guess that their leave expired in precisely forty-eight hours, and that if they were late they would be left behind?

And yet, they always *did* know. Some strange feline jungle telegraph sent its mysterious messages through the back streets and alleys of Naples or Malta or Mauritius, or wherever the ship might be, and out came the pussies shortly before sailing time, padding silently along towards the docks, greeting one another — one likes to think — with stories of adventure and romance. Sometimes they cut things very fine, so that the last gangway would be on the point of being raised when the last pussy rushed aboard. But they always knew, so the admiral swore, and I was brought up to believe that admirals never tell a lie.

The affection of sailors should be enough to dispel the legend that the cat is only the old maids' darling, but history abounds in examples of many other brave men whose hearts have warmed to a purr and melted to a mew. Abraham Lincoln is not normally regarded as a missish type, and yet, during one of the most anxious moments of the Civil War, he had time to spare to save three deserted kittens from starvation. The episode occurred in General Grant's camp. Lincoln stumbled upon them in a deserted tent. The campaign was in a crucial stage, his heart must have been burdened with crushing cares, but Lincoln lifted up the kittens and smuggled them under his coat and did not leave them till he had seen that they would be properly cared for.

But why quote further examples of pussy's eminent friends? After all, we decided that O should stand for Old Maids. And even if cats had been created solely for them, their role would be important enough. To bring solace to the lonely and gaiety to the ageing, to give to each separate day a constant variety and to life, as a whole, a soft purring rhythm ... could we, with reason, ask for more?

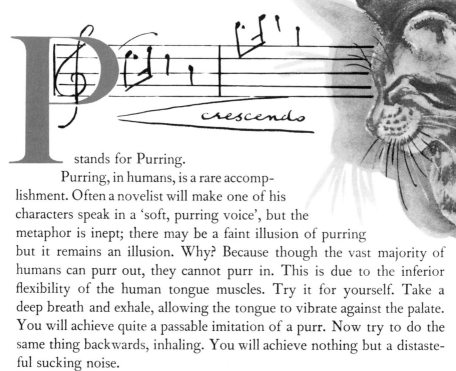

P stands for Purring.

Purring, in humans, is a rare accomplishment. Often a novelist will make one of his characters speak in a 'soft, purring voice', but the metaphor is inept; there may be a faint illusion of purring but it remains an illusion. Why? Because though the vast majority of humans can purr out, they cannot purr in. This is due to the inferior flexibility of the human tongue muscles. Try it for yourself. Take a deep breath and exhale, allowing the tongue to vibrate against the palate. You will achieve quite a passable imitation of a purr. Now try to do the same thing backwards, inhaling. You will achieve nothing but a distasteful sucking noise.

I once met a man with an almost perfect purr, in as well as out. He was an admiral of the fleet, and he was staying with the Governor of Gibraltar, with whom I was dining. How we began to talk about purring I cannot recollect, but you may imagine my delight when I discovered that so distinguished a man was gifted with so exceptional a talent. There he sat, in the candlelight, fingering the stem of his wine-glass, purring with supreme virtuosity. His uniform was ablaze with decorations, and I remember thinking how ironic it was that none of them had been awarded for purring.

When I was planning this little volume I wrote to the admiral asking if I might mention him by name. He replied, politely but firmly, that he would prefer to remain anonymous. He seemed to imagine that his gift, if widely known, might lead to adverse comment on the lower deck. I cannot believe that this was his true reason; I suspect that he really feared that it might make the other admirals jealous.

Hassan, my Indian bearer during the latter part of the war, was another man with an authentic two-way purr. This was by no means his only claim to originality; he had, for example, a remarkable flair for dress. Soon after I had engaged him, I was bidden to stay with the Viceroy at Delhi, and I told Hassan that he must smarten himself up if he wished to accompany me. The Viceroy's servants, I remembered, were very grand in scarlet and gold, and Hassan looked like a sort of pirate. So I gave him money to get a new outfit. For two days he disappeared, and I was about to give him up as a bad job, and engage another man, when suddenly he came back, looking more like a pirate than ever. His method of getting a new outfit had been to search the bazaars and the junk-shops for a mass of military decorations, badges, ribbons, cap-bands, stripes and symbols of every description, which he had proudly sewn on to his jacket. I pretended to be annoyed, though I was in fact enchanted, and to put me in a good humour — for he knew I loved cats — he suddenly lowered his head and began to purr, a deep, rich purr in and out, of impeccable felinity. He was a great success with the Viceroy, who informed me that nothing quite like him had ever entered the portals of Vice-regal Lodge before, which I can well believe.

Hassan eventually purred himself out of my life in Madras, accompanied by my cuff links, my cigarette case and a large wad of rupees which he had abstracted from my wallet in a fit of absent-mindedness. It was an expensive purr, but it was worth it.

The most exquisite purr I have known, a real prima donna of a purr, belongs to my own cat 'Four'. It has all the qualities which connoisseurs of purring esteem most highly ... a perfect *vibrato*, superb breath control, exquisite quality of tone and a quite exceptional range, which stretches from a rich contralto to a flawless E in alt. There is no role where purring is demanded which 'Four' could not play with the greatest distinction. Moreover, 'Four' needs no human encouragement to make him perform; like all great artists he purrs for the sake of purring. Often, when I have been sitting at my desk, without knowing that he was near me, I have been suddenly startled by the fluting sounds of 'Four's' purr, and I look down to see him gazing at me ... rather in the manner of a prima donna who is waiting for her accompanist.

'Five' has a gentle, pleasing purr, but he would be the last to describe himself as a great artist; he excels in other spheres. Oscar has talent and energy but his purr is undisciplined and his enthusiasm runs away with him. As we noted in a previous chapter, he is inclined, out of sheer emotion, to dribble. This usually occurs when I am having breakfast in bed, and I have discovered a simple way of stopping it. (The student who has read D for Dilapidations will recall that Oscar had a regrettably Bohemian upbringing.) To interrupt him in the middle of an aria would be unkind and humiliating, so I usually allow him to have his purr out, and in the meantime I tactfully slide a copy of the *Financial Times* under him, to deal with the dribbles. The perusal of this journal, throughout my life, has been so uniformly depressing that I am glad to be able to put it to some practical use.

All Fs will have their own pet varieties of the exquisite art of purring. Some prefer their purrs pianissimo ... the sort of faint, sweet song that comes from a kettle that one leaves on the hob, by a log fire. Some demand greater volume, and will go to any lengths of stroking and cosseting to produce loud and brilliant purrs which will arouse envy in the hearts of other Fs, whose pussies are not so accomplished. But nearly all will agree that the best purr of all, the purr that speaks most directly to the heart, is the first faint purr that comes from a frightened stray, that one has found in the rain and taken in one's arms and coaxed with confidence. This is the purr that is quite irresistible, the language that only a brute would fail to heed.

Q stands for Query.

The mind of the cat is a jungle abounding in marks of interrogation, through which Fs can find their way by instinct, while non-Fs flounder and are lost and frightened. Why should this be? Why is the world divided — as it evidently is — into two classes, F and non-F? Here is a suitable moment for examining this fascinating problem.

Let me state at the outset that I do not regard the non-F's dislike of cats as an affectation. If a man shrinks back in horror as soon as 'Five' walks into the room, and stares at him as though he were some dreadful apparition from Outer Space, I am prepared to concede that he is really expressing a genuine emotion, and not putting on an act. All I would observe, in passing, is that some non-Fs seem to be rather proud of their non-Fness, as though it were in some way associated with the heroic virtues. But is it? When females are being rescued from burning buildings is the doggy man always the first up the ladder, while the cat-lover slinks away, in craven shame, into the shadows? No doubt some would say so. But I would like some rather more definite proof.

The popular novelists are largely responsible for this artificial division of human and animal nature, in which all the broad-shouldered, blue-eyed V.C.s are put in one pen, smoking pipes and surrounded by adoring cocker spaniels, while all the decadents are put in another, inhaling Turkish cigarettes and muttering sinister things to Siamese kittens. In spite of Freud, much of the psychology of the modern best-seller is still so shallow that when a novelist wishes to darken the character of one of his puppets all he has to do is to cause a dog to snarl at him, the assumption being that the dog has a sort of psychic nose for evil. This is really rather unfair; if it were true a great many of us would be revealed in a most unbecoming light — including myself. For many years my visits to the house of a devoted friend were complicated, to put it mildly, by the presence of two gigantic Alsatians who obviously regarded me with the utmost disfavour. They were the size of Shetland ponies, they had gleaming yellow fangs, and their barks, echoing through the long gallery of the entrance hall, were so deafening and so prolonged that for the first ten minutes after arriving one had to shout to make oneself heard. They never actually bit me but one day, to my great satisfaction, they bit a fellow guest, twice, on the behind. And he *had* broad shoulders, and he *had* blue eyes, and he *was* a V.C. Which 'only goes to show', as my old nanny used to observe.

But no novelist would ever permit his hero, and a V.C. at that, to be bitten on the behind by an Alsatian, or even by a rather petulant Borzoi. Scratched by a cat — yes, *that* would accord with all the manly virtues, and might even be interpeted as a token of virility; bitten by a dog — no, it would be totally out of character, like being kicked by a horse. And now that we are on this subject, let us consider this question of horses. (In modern Britain, one is indeed compelled to consider them. The shadow of the horse looms so large over British society that one wonders why the *Court Circular* is not renamed the *Equine Gazette*.)

As I have a distinct partiality for almost anything on four legs, I can claim a quite genuine affection for horses, provided that they are old and solid, with shaggy manes, in a pleasing shade of Rembrandt brown, and leaning over rustic gates. Otherwise, I must confess, I can dispense with horses. Quite frankly, they alarm me. I think that the noise they make through their nostrils, on occasions, is positively macabre, and I do not care whether it is *joie de vivre*, rage, or simply acute sinus; it terrifies me. Also, they kick, hard. And they look as though they bite, and I suspect that they do, though I have never really explored this question. On the very few occasions when I have stayed at grand houses where people have stables, and when we have gone off to 'see the horses' before luncheon, I have usually managed to slink off and strike up an acquaintance with the stable cat.

All this has taken us a long way from our original question. *Why* is mankind divided into two classes, F and non-F? Maybe there is no final answer to this question. And yet, some years ago, in a French scientific journal whose name I have forgotten — (I picked it up in the waiting-room of a doctor in the rue de Lille) — I read a theory that seemed to make sense. Apparently some doctor in Toulouse had made an experiment with several hundred babies of all descriptions, male, female, white, brown and black, ranging in age from three to eighteen months. These creatures were disposed in perambulators, and various French pussies were introduced to them. Nine per cent of the infants, even before they had seen the pussies, went into brisk convulsions providing that pussy was to the windward of them; if pussy was on the other side there was no reaction. The obvious assumption was that non-Fness is in some manner connected with the sense of smell — an assumption that would vindicate the claim made by some Fs that they are aware of the presence of a cat in a room even if it is for the moment invisible.

To Fs, this will seem a curious excuse for non-Fness. Compared with most animals, the cat is singularly inoffensive. Indeed, I have a distinct partiality for the odour of fur, particularly after pussy has been performing her ablutions; it has the same faint fragrance that comes from damp moss, which is a great deal more than one can say for most human beings.

So perhaps we had better leave the question unanswered. There are Fs and non-Fs; we will leave it at that. But I do not see that we need necessarily assume that never the twain shall meet. All we would suggest is that at least we meet on a level of equality.

82

R stands for *rubato* or *rallentando* …
though any other musical expression would serve as well. For here we shall discuss cats and music, beginning with the first introduction of the new kitten to the wonders of the grand pianoforte.

Looking back on my life, a large part of it seems to have been spent on my knees, coaxing kittens from under sofas in music-rooms, after they have been unnecessarily alarmed by my rendering of Chopin's second Scherzo. If this were indeed the case, my life would have been well conducted, for there could surely be no pleasanter combination of circumstances than Chopin, a music-room, and a new kitten. However, my memory is probably exaggerating; memory often does, when it is summoning up the ghosts of past delights. How many golden hours one seems to be able to recall, lying on the burning sands of the Mediterranean! When one adds them up they really amount to a few weeks in Cannes, which were usually marked by a series of cloudbursts.

To return to the kitten and the piano, it is vitally important, at the beginning of the operation, that the kitten should be in a mood of complete relaxation. All nervous tensions must have been eased. Pingpong balls must have been replaced in drawers, pieces of screwed-up paper must have been removed from sight. The kitten's tummy, if possible, should be full. The mood should be one of luxury and repletion, and it should be enhanced by a judicious application of the various arts of stroking, which are fully enunciated under the letter S.

These physical conditions having been ensured, the kitten may be lifted up, like a ball in the palm of the hand, and gently placed on a bound copy of the Sonatas of Mozart, which is lying on top of the piano. Here, we are perhaps being unduly perfectionist. No great crisis will ensue if one places the kitten on an unbound copy of the Sonatas of Beethoven — or, for that matter, on any solid volume of classical music. What would happen if one were to place it on a volume of jazz I do not know, for the simple reason that such an object has not, so far, been admitted to my house.

One may now take one's seat at the piano, put one's foot on the soft pedal, and very gently strike the note G in alt. Here again we may be accused of undue perfectionism; G♭ would do as well, or G♯; the point to be observed is that the note should be reasonably high and extremely soft. A loud note in the bass would immediately suggest growls, and the kitten's musical education might suffer a serious setback.

The effect of this first note will vary according to the kitten's temperament. On some it may be nearly disastrous — there may be a wild leap from the piano on to the floor, and a frenzied escape into the garden, if one has been so unwise as to leave the door open. In such cases, there will be a long and difficult road ahead, in which one continues to strike G in alt, day after day, until the kitten is at last convinced that one is not invoking the voice of the devil.

Such cases, fortunately, are few and far between. More often the reaction is roughly as follows:

First G.   Saucer eyes, swift glances to the right and left, and a step backward.

Second G.   Wider saucer eyes, more glances, and a step forward.

Third G.   Widest of all saucer eyes, crouching, and several steps forward to the edge of the piano.

When this stage is reached, the F may use his own discretion. There will, of course, be more strokings, and more soothing and melodious words. In my own experience I have found it helpful, before striking G for the fourth time, to tap the wire of the note with my fingernail; and then, if this arouses interest, to draw the nail gently across several wires — an action which produces a pleasing and faintly plaintive sound which is not unfeline in quality.

The vital point, as always, is to try to enter into pussy's mind and to shrink oneself to pussy's proportions, so that one can imagine how it feels to be hoisted on to a black shiny mountain and transported to the edge of a dark cavern, from whose interior strange wails and howls are echoing. Most humans, in such circumstances, would probably go nearly mad, and spend the rest of their lives being psycho-analysed.

We now enter the realm of traveller's tales. I would not care to make a definite assertion that cats are musical, but I have a strong suspicion that they are not unmusical, by which I mean that ugly sounds distress them. My own cats, quite definitely, dislike the various forms of cacophony which, in these days, are lumped under the generic name of 'jazz'. Even in the best regulated households, these sounds sometimes intrude, in spite of all the precautions that may be taken against them. Young people come to dine, bearing with them these shining, sinister discs of discord; they drift over to the gramophone and put them on and jig about the room to the resultant uproar. One likes young people, one tries to be a good host, and one has the faint hope that one may not yet be quite old enough to be cast for the role of Scrooge. So one allows the uproar to continue.

But it is with some satisfaction that one notes that 'Four' has risen from the chair in which he was comfortably asleep, and is stalking from the room with some hauteur, casting a look of unmitigated disgust at the instrument from which the horrible sounds are pouring.

'Four' has never left the room when I am playing Chopin and sometimes I dare to think that one green eye opens, and regards me with approval, when the slow movement of the Grieg Concerto is going rather better than usual. However that may be, cats and music have always been linked in my mind, and always will be. The basket of kittens in the nursery — and the exercises by Stephen Heller; the incredibly old Blüthner in the drawing-room of my boyhood, and the incredibly old black cat who used to sit on top of it; pianos galore, cats galore. Even in the concert hall … even, I dare to say it, during the music of Mozart … ghostly felines have a way of drifting across the stage, for Mozart, as we have previously observed, was F from tip to toe. (I nearly wrote from tip to tail.) And so was Chopin and so was Brahms, and so were Delius and Tschaikowski and César Franck and … But I seem to be drifting back to my foreword. The one thing we must never forget is that Wagner was non-F. He was a great black dog, growling in the bass and howling to the moon.

S stands for Stroking.

Stroking is a delicate art, whose subtleties are little understood by non-Fs. Even some Fs have much to learn about it. In any properly organized society there would be State schools to teach the elements of deportment towards felines. In such schools, stroking would be one of the most important of all the students' courses.

Several volumes might — and certainly should — be written about the charming occupation of cat-stroking. After all, this is a perfect example of an occasion when the human and animal kingdoms are united in complete harmony, a harmony which is expressed by the music of the purr. However, as space is restricted, we must be content with a few generalizations.

Surprising as it may seem, there is only one form of stroking which is acceptable at *all* times in *all* circumstances by *all* felines. This is …

(A) *The Under-the-Chin Stroke*. The importance of this form of stroking may be very simply tested. Supposing that the student is walking down a street, and is lucky enough to encounter a cat sitting on a wall. He will naturally desire to strike up an acquaintance even — or in some cases especially — if the cat is battered and tough, with, in all probability, a touch of cynicism. If he walks straight up and tries to stroke it on the back, he may quite rightly receive a scratch for his pains. After all, he is a stranger and his motives may be suspect; he has not yet established a stroking relationship nor created a stroking atmosphere.

How then must the student conduct himself? Very slowly and gently, so that pussy may follow his every movement, he must advance his hand, with the wrist in an advanced position. Here he must pause to study pussy's reactions. If they are favourable he may advance his hand further, with the wrist still forward, and only when the wrist is almost touching pussy's chin should he extend the fingers and begin the stroking movement.

As soon as contact has been established, the stroking may proceed with increasing energy. Accomplished Fs will not need to be told that this is a moment when many pleasing variations may be introduced. Of these perhaps the most technically difficult is the clenched fist stroke, which explains itself — the fist is tightly clenched and the knuckles are rubbed briskly, indeed almost violently, on the side of the chin. Some cats, whose experience of professional stroking is unfortunately limited, may at first express surprise at this development, but it will only be a matter of a few seconds before they begin to co-operate.

(B) *The Back Stroke.* This is, of course, the conventional form of stroking, familiar to F and non-F alike — and alas, in the hands of the latter, what a very bourgeois and uninspiring exercise it usually proves to be! A few casual dabs at pussy's back and a feeble twiddly scratching of pussy's head. No subtlety of finger work, no attempt at *vibrato*, no sense of rhythm. To watch a non-F engaged in back-stroking is to be reminded of the essential crudity of the human race.

Fs will agree that the apparent simplicity of back-stroking is highly deceptive. It is like the music of Mozart which looks so easy that you would think a child could play it, whereas, in fact, it demands an impeccable technique. Indeed, the task of the back-stroker is even more difficult than the task of the musician. Once one has mastered, let us say, the Adagio of the eighteenth sonata in D major one can play it on any piano, provided that the instrument is in tune; all keyboards are identical. But no cats are identical; their backs vary in size, shape, texture and resilience; with each new cat one must begin, in every sense of the phrase, from scratch.

Only a few elemental examples can here be offered as a guide to those non-Fs who, let us hope, have learned the error of their ways and wish to join the ranks of civilized — i.e. advanced back-stroking — society.

Since we have used the musical metaphor, we will continue it. To begin with, we would suggest ...

1. *The Andante Stroke.* This is a slow, simple movement in which the principal agent is the palm of the hand. The stroke should begin at the base of the neck and stop approximately two inches before the tail. The phrasing should be, of course, legato, and the tempo should be a strict 2/4 to the bar.

This stroke may be used, with mutual pleasure and profit, on tranquil occasions when pussy is sitting in front of a log fire, when the room is filled with the fragrance of apple wood, and when the golden shadows on the ceiling are like the blossoms of ghostly laburnums, swaying in the wind.

2. *Staccato con brio.* This is a highly effective stroke, which may at first appear to the non-F as beyond his technical capacity. However, in spite of its superficial brilliance, it is not as difficult as might be imagined. One could compare it, in this respect, to that old concert chestnut 'The Rustle of Spring', whose facile arpeggios have dazzled generations of simple audiences in village halls.

The *staccato con brio* stroke should be reserved for festive occasions, when the mood is gay and dancing, and is perhaps best practised in the open air. Both hands are used, in order to execute a series of swift staccato scales, beginning on the crown of the head and ending with a brilliant passage down the tail. Lightness of touch is absolutely essential. If the student does not feel quite happy about his rendering of this stroke, he would be well advised to spend a few weeks at the pianoforte, perfecting some of the more elaborate cadenzas of Liszt.

(C) *Tummy-Rubbing.* There appear to be three schools of feline thought about tummy-rubbing.

Members of the first school are quite evidently bored by the whole procedure. Although they may assume a tummy-rubbing posture, and dispose themselves on the hearth-rug with both paws languidly crossed over their chests, as soon as the tummy-rubbing begins their faces register intense ennui,

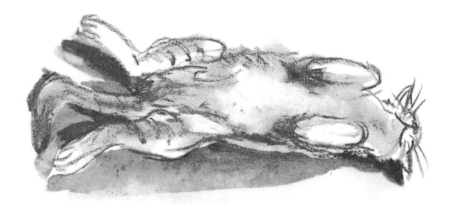

and they regard the tummy-rubber with cold contemptuous eyes, as if demanding that he should immediately cease this nonsense, and turn his fingers to some more profitable exercise.

Members of the second school of thought are actively hostile. At the first suggestion of tummy-rubbing they will 'back-pedal' violently, as a signal that they are not amused.

Members of the third school, however — approximately seventy per cent of the feline world — find a certain amount of intelligent tummy-rubbing essential to their peace of mind. The accent is on the word intelligent. Tummy-rubbing is not to be performed as though one were brushing a hearth-rug. Only the tips of the fingers should be used. As a rough guide the tempo is 4/4 and the mood is *andante moderato*. (In the case of Siamese, omit the *moderato*.) The movement should be spiral, and from time to time, if the tummy-rubbing is proceeding smoothly, the tail may be very delicately pulled.

A Note on Stroking Neuters

The sensation of being stroked on the back, in the case of some neuters, is so exceedingly agreeable that it causes them to assume postures which might possibly be regarded as inelegant. My own cat 'Four', for example, if firmly stroked, crouches on his front legs and elevates his behind so sharply that his whole body is hoisted at an angle of forty-five degrees. Moreover, having adopted this attitude, he is apt to remain in it for several minutes, even after the stroking has stopped. On occasions this habit has caused embarrassment to visitors. They enter a room, they observe a feline apparently transfixed in what seems to them a singular attitude, and they jump to extraordinary conclusions.

I cannot offer the student any absolutely infallible advice in this dilemma, apart from the suggestion that he should announce that he is not at home to visitors. However, if the posture strikes him as exaggerated, he may slightly modify it by combining back-stroking with chin-stroking; this will normally cause pussy's posterior to sink by about five degrees. He may also, in extreme cases, give pussy a gentle push on to the carpet. In this position there are various other technical devices by which he may gradually soften pussy's ardour, such as nose-rubbing and a very gentle variation of the afore-mentioned *staccato con brio*.

I must apologize if the foregoing paragraphs give a slightly non-F impression. I need hardly say that the true F will find nothing unnatural or embarrassing in the sight of a cat whose behind is hoisted at such a precipitous angle. However, I am aware that non-Fs are basically anthropomorphic, and are apt to translate pussy's reactions into human terms, so that they unconsciously see themselves, or their female friends, sitting on the carpet in a similar position. I should be the first to agree that this would be, indeed, a most distasteful spectacle.

T stands for Trivia.

It might have stood for Toms or Tails or Tabbies. Indeed, I was actually pondering which of these important subjects to discuss; when something happened. A single crimson petal from a bowl of peonies dropped lazily on to the rug in front of the fire-place. At the same time 'Four' darted out from under the sofa, and flicked the petal with his paw, so that it was tossed up into a shaft of sunlight. And I realized that this was one of those flashes of happiness that I shall recall for the rest of my life. Not because there was anything strange or spectacular about it, but because cats have an extraordinary capacity for making single moments seem dramatic, so that they linger for ever in one's memory. I feel that a cat must have been in the room when Rupert Brooke wrote:

> One instant I, an instant, knew,
> As God knows all. And it and you
> I, above Time, oh, blind! could see
> In witless immortality.
> I saw the marble cup; the tea,
> Hung on the air, an amber stream;
> I saw the fire's unglittering gleam,
> The painted flame, the frozen smoke ...

So it was on this occasion. I shall remember the peony petal and the way it glowed, for a brief second, as it caught the sun. I shall remember putting down my pen, and staring at the petal, and listening to the song of a thrush singing in the dark branches of the copper beech. I shall remember, too, how my mind set off, not for the first time, on the least fruitful of all philosophical explorations, examining the pros and cons of predestation. If the Universe is not to be regarded as a senseless chaos, if there is indeed a master plan, in which no detail is left to chance, then from the beginning of time it must have been ordained that my peony petal should fall at precisely that moment. Moons have waxed and waned, winds have driven across the earth, waters have ebbed and swollen, seeds and roots have struggled for survival, through countless centuries, simply in order to achieve the desired result of a single petal falling, a black cat leaping, and a shaft of sunlight catching a patch of crimson.

If this is not the case, if the petal fell by blind chance, then anything can fall by chance, including those comforting sparrows. Houses can fall by chance, and bombs and meteors ... and oh dear me this is all getting too depressing. It is the fault of 'Four', who is something of a philosopher himself, and firmly on the side of predestation when it is a matter of fish.

I wonder if there are any other people, with reasonable claims to sanity, whose minds attach little feline tags to all sorts of unsuitable objects. Consider the question of furniture. I happen to be fond of paying my half-crown and prowling round old houses where there are fine examples of eighteenth-century walnut, and constantly when I have been examining a Chippendale chair or a Hepplewhite bureau I have been startled by seeing, or seeming to see, a ghostly paw protruding between the legs. This is because there stands by the side of my desk a charming Chippendale waste-paper basket, in a sort of open Chinese latticework, through which Oscar frequently puts his paw in order to dab at the crumpled pieces of paper inside. On one occasion Oscar developed such a passionate interest in the waste-paper basket, sniffing it, and poking his paws in it and standing on his hind legs against it, that for an awful moment I feared that it might be sheltering some unfortunate refugee in the shape of a mouse. Investigation proved it to be not a mouse but an olive stone, which somebody had dropped into the basket after a cocktail party. Oscar has a morbid craving for olives, and before any party they have to be kept firmly locked up in the pantry.

There's another fascinating topic for all trivia ... cats and food. In any place where cat-lovers are gathered together, sooner or later the subject of food will be eagerly discussed, with particular emphasis on any pussy who has peculiar tastes. (My own contribution, on these occasions, is the story of one of my earliest cats, who was called Beresford. He had a passion for the pulpy inside of melons.) Often there is a strong streak of masochism in these stories. 'My dear,' exclaims an excited lady, '*can* you guess what that wicked Tibby did last night? John had somebody *terribly* important to dinner and I bought a jar of caviare from Fortnum's — not the red sort but the *enormous* grey sort — and Tibby gobbled the lot just before dinner!' This story causes her confidante to shudder with delight and embark on some story to prove that her own pussy is capable of equally outrageous behaviour. Let us be honest, most of us rather like our cats to have a streak of wickedness. I should not feel quite easy in the company of any cat that walked about the house with a saintly expression, never scratching the chairs.

That word 'scratching' sets one's mind off again, into the lumber-room of memory ... and what a host of trivia it discovers! But are they all trivia? I wonder. Let me tell you a story. In my last winter at Merry Hall, a house which I greatly loved, I had to cut down an old pear tree. This is a horrible thing to have to do, at any time; it is a form of murder; but in this case it was particularly distasteful because it happened to be a tree which had been a favourite of my Siamese cat 'One', who had often climbed up in its branches. So when the tree was being cut down I went away for the week-end, which may strike some people as showing an excess of sensibility. I do not greatly care.

Came the spring — a cold, acid spring which made great demands on the central heating. I said to Gaskin: 'We'd better start on the logs from that old pear tree; they should burn by now.' So the logs were brought into the music-room, and I laid a fire of bits and pieces and set the first branch of pear wood on the top.

Then, as the flames began to flicker round it, I noticed something strange about the bark. It was flecked and scarred with a thousand tiny marks. Suddenly, I realized the significance of those marks. They were the signs of 'One's' scratching. I had never known that this was his special scratching tree, for its bark had always been hidden by a thick growth of shrubs, but so it must have been. Year in and year out he must have wandered out on his mysterious errands, and pushed his way through the jungle of the shrubbery, stretched out his paws and tautened his back and indulged in this strange rite of scratching. And in the end, 'One' had sickened and lost his hold on life ... this was two years before ... and I had been compelled to arrange for him to be put away.

Two deaths — the death of a faithful friend and the death of a tree. And for both of them I had been responsible. The flames flickered and curled round the log, slowly the scratch marks were darkened, and then there was only flame and smoke, drifting up the chimney. There was a terrible finality about that moment, as though a chapter in my life were closing, indeed, a whole series of chapters.

T for Trivia? Again, I wonder. For if a scratch on a tree can make one feel that the whole world is in mourning, what happens when one is confronted by the real tragedies of life?

stands for
Under the Walnut Tree.
This title, I confess, is
sheer cheating. But what is one to do? I wanted to write about battle
and conflict among cats — all the strange pomps and circumstances of
feline War, all the mysterious physical and psychic influences that suddenly cause their backs to arch, their legs to stiffen, and their bodies to
be switched into that extraordinary and very frightening position in which
pussy is broadside on, with a fierce and bristling tail at the alert.

But there were no letters left to fit these grim occasions. B, which
might have stood for Battle, had already been annexed for the comparatively gentle art of Beeing, as you may remember. As for the letter W,
which might have stood for War ... that had already been reserved for a
thesis on Weaving.

And yet, there is some slight justification for this technical trick.
For in my new garden — which is in fact a very old garden and, I hope, my
last — there is an immense walnut tree, whose branches have been moulded
by time into a design of muscular beauty. In the shade of this walnut tree
the first conflicts have been waged between 'Four', 'Five' and Oscar on
the one hand, and Rudolph and Pemberton on the other. (They are the
cats next door.) In this same shade, sentry watch is undertaken, and major
decisions of strategy decided.

When I first encountered Rudolph and Pemberton, I had a dim
hope that they might make friends with my own family. They were both
of the greatest amiability, very sleek and plump, one ginger and one
tabby. Before we moved in, they had an engaging habit of walking up the
little path of the cottage, and strolling in through the front door, as
though the place belonged to them. In the life-time of the previous
owner, apparently, they had been made welcome, and given fish — not

that they really needed it — and encouraged to leap on beds. I thought how pleasant it would be to continue this admirable tradition.

I was a fool, of course. On the very first night that 'Four', 'Five' and Oscar were given their latchkeys — by which I mean the first night on which we felt it would be safe to open the cat-doors — I was woken in the small hours by the familiar cacophony, rising and falling, ebbing and swelling, drifting through the open window. Not that I find the sound of caterwauling, in itself, distasteful; indeed, compared with the noise emitted by the average television crooner it is as sweet as the breath of lutes and the sigh of harps, echoing down some Elysian valley. All that worries me when I hear caterwauling is the knowledge that the woodwind motif, as it were, may suddenly give way to a passage of percussion, and lead to scratched noses and bitten ears.

Which was precisely what happened at this moment. The woodwind rose to incredible heights in minor thirds, gained steadily in volume, and suddenly broke, literally, into percussion as a flower-pot was knocked off a window ledge to the accompaniment of a fusillade of hisses, punctuated by a few *ad lib.* cadenzas in alt. I sprang to the window, and shouted and clapped my hands, and made all the usual futile noises. Dark shapes flitted away from under the chequered shadows of the walnut tree and once again there was silence.

But war had been declared, and I fear that it continues to this day.

Why do cats fight?

Why do two beautiful bundles of fur, who might wander off together, exchanging sniffs and purrs and confidences, immediately transform themselves into a pair of crook-backed, howling demons of destruction?

Once again, I think that this is a problem which might be firmly deposited, like the problem of the cat and the mouse, on the lap of the Almighty. And having done so, we might turn to address a few words to the non-F, who is inclined to reach for the nearest brick at the least sign of feline conflict.

'At least' ... so we should address the non-F ... 'the battles of cats are far less deplorable, far less morally reprehensible, than the battles of men.'

When cats fight they fight as individuals, driven by the storms and stresses of Nature, in whose soul there is always conflict. They do not march in serried lines, like an exceptionally stupid breed of sheep, to the command of a cackle from a radio.

Legions of tabbies do not suddenly advance across Richmond Bridge in order to destroy legions of Siamese, lined up on the opposite bank, merely because some pampered Persian ... whom none of them has ever met ... has ordered them to do so. Well, they don't, do they? Yet this is precisely what men do.

Battalions of black cats from the East End do not suddenly lose their reason, and band together, and charge up Park Lane in order to battle to the death with opposing battalions of white cats from the West End, merely because some cat in the suburbs ... who was probably a dingy shade of brown, anyway ... has thought up some idiotic slogan about the supremacy of white (or black) races. Yet that is precisely what men do.

From all of this we may conclude that pussy, waging her intensely personal conflicts in the shadow of the walnut tree, presents a somewhat less ugly picture than Man, waging his coldly impersonal conflicts on whatever battlefield may be the vogue at the moment. All the same, I regret these feline conflicts. Even when hostilities are not actually in progress, they are in the air. And always they centre round the walnut, for the branches of this ancient tree spread far across the outbuildings, casting their shade over the roof of the old tool-shed, and this roof has been chosen by 'Four', 'Five' and Oscar as a sort of outpost, from which they may repel any sorties from Rudolph and Pemberton.

Even as I write, they are sitting there like sentries, silent, immobile except for an occasional lashing of the tail, eternally at the alert. And there, on the opposite wall, sit Rudolph and Pemberton, also silent, also immobile ... except for the aforesaid tail lashing. And I walk up the little staircase and look out of the crooked window and heave a sigh and think how idiotic it all is. They might be playing together, they might be s niffing and dabbing and chasing each other. But no, they do no such thing. They only sit and glare. One would think they had all been reading the morning's edition of the *Daily Worker*.

V stands for Verses.

Inevitably, pussy has inspired a great deal of poetry throughout the ages, and inevitably most of it is very bad indeed. (Though not nearly as bad as the poems which have been inspired by dogs.) Oddly enough, most of the really atrocious feline verse has been written by men ... strong and usually silent men, too. Large, muscular Christians, living impeccable lives in cathedral closes, have gazed into pussy's eyes, gasped with delight, and burst into verses of incredible archness. They have gurgled about pussy's toes and tinkled about her tail and shuddered with ecstasy as she weaves around their gaiters. The women have been comparatively restrained and have managed to keep their humour, like the American lady who wrote

> O lovely bit
> Of silky fur
> Jewel-eyed
> Aristocrat
> I'd wear you
> To the Opera
> If you were
> Not my cat.

From time to time, however, a great poet has looked into the eyes of a cat, and a spark has been lit, and a flame of beauty has shone across a page. Here, of course, I must quote Blake's 'Tyger! Tyger! burning bright, in the forests of the night'. The word 'burning', in such a context,

is breath-taking — the quintessence of inspiration. It must have lit on Blake's pen like a flash of lightning from the night sky.

Every schoolboy knows the first couplet of the Tyger. (Even as I wrote this I was struck by the awful thought that there may be some horrid little creatures who do *not* know it.) But the rest of the poem may not be so familiar. The climax has always seemed to me to come in the fourth verse, after Blake has flung the immortal question 'In what distant deeps or skies, burnt the fire of thine eyes?'

What the hammer? What the chain?
In what furnace was thy brain?
What the anvil? What dread grasp
Dare its deadly terrors clasp?

Sometimes when I have been looking into the green mystery of 'Four's' eyes, and have marvelled at the way the dark band of the iris turns and thickens as he turns his head, I have seemed to see deeper and ever deeper, as though I were exploring some green corridor that stretched into infinity, and I have fancied that I caught a faint glow of red from Blake's furnace. But I have never been able to look long enough to make quite sure. 'Four' always stares me out, and compels me to lower my eyes. That is one very notable difference between dogs and cats. Often, if you stare into the eyes of a dog, he will look away in embarrassment, as though he knew that he was inferior. A cat will never do this. She will always stare back, because she knows that she is one's equal, if not one's superior.

Swinburne was one of the poets who noted this fact. Most of us only know Swinburne as the lyric virtuoso of his early poems, with their dazzling rhymes and alliterations ... poems in which there is always an

echo of the sea, a tidal surge and a foam of spray. But he was in a very different mood when he wrote a poem to his cat.

> Stately, kindly, lordly friend
> Condescend
> Here to sit by me, and turn
> Glorious eyes that smile and burn.
>
> Dogs may fawn on all and some
> As they come
> You, a friend of loftier mind
> Answer friends alone in kind
> Just your foot upon my hand
> Softly bids it understand.

The non-F may interpret this charming verse as an attack on dogs. It is, of course, nothing of the sort. Swinburne was devoted to many dogs; he was merely observing that the cat is at least the dog's *social* superior. That is why the cat, unlike the dog, will always stare back at a human instead of lowering its eyes. The old saying that 'a cat may look at a queen' is sound natural history.

This proud gaze of the feline has been noted in a very moving poem by an English writer, Ruth Pitter. It is called 'To a Caged Lion', and the first verse runs ...

> You are afraid. You do not dare
> Up to the lion to lift your eyes,
> And unashamed his beauty share
> As once in that lost paradise.

Poet after poet has celebrated the strange aura of past glory that seems to glow round the heads of cats, the indefinable air of aristocracy, of ancient freedom, that makes one feel that there must be royal blood in the veins of even the scruffiest pussy in the alley. Many of the poets, too,

have guessed that pussy is conscious of her heritage, and spends much of her life consoling herself for the sorrows of the present by recalling the splendours of the past. Time and again they invoke the image of the Sphinx, as in Baudelaire's *Les Fleurs du Mal* ...

> Ils prennent en songeant les nobles attitudes
> Des grands sphinx allongés au fond des solitudes
> Qui semblent s'endormir dans un rêve sans fin.

However, most of our social intercourse with pussy is, fortunately, on not so lofty a level; otherwise we should be for ever bowing and curtseying to one another, and stepping back at doorways to offer precedence. That is why I think the poets rather overdo their favourite feline theme of the cat's ancient royal lineage. The theme is a true one, but it is not the only one, and sometimes poor pussy -- starved, neglected, terrified by the cruelty of the world, is hard put to it to remember her royal antecedents.

Thomas Hardy must have realized this when he wrote a poem mourning the death of his own cat ... a poem which has a greater dignity and depth of feeling than many epitaphs for men and women.

From the chair whereon he sat
Sweep his fur, nor wince thereat;
Rake his little pathways out
Mid the bushes roundabout;
Smooth away his talons' mark
From the claw-worn pine-tree bark,
Where he climbed as dusk embrowned,
Waiting us who loitered round.

Strange it is this speechless thing
Subject to our mastering,
Subject for his life and food
To our gift, and time, and mood;
Timid pensioner of us Powers,
His existence ruled by ours,
Should — by crossing at a breath
Into safe and shielded death,
By the merely taking hence
Of his insignificance —
Loom as part, above man's will
Of the Imperturbable.

Strange indeed it is. Strange .., and in some way comforting. 'Safe and shielded death.' The last gift that not even the cruelty of man can deny.

W

stands for Weaving.

'Weaving' is the name we give to charming curving movements which cats make round our legs when they are feeling more than usually friendly or when, to be frank, the fish is boiling and the kitchen is filled with a piscine aroma. I know of no other animal capable of performing these convolutions, which never fail to delight me — or perhaps I should have written, almost never, for there have been times when the weaving proclivities of 'Five' have made me late for a party. No sooner have I got into my dinner jacket than 'Five' appears, obviously drenched with affection, and sweeps round my legs, leaving my trousers covered with white and grey hair. 'You should not let him come near you when you are dressed for dinner,' says Gaskin severely, as he brushes my trousers. Which may be true but is not very helpful.

There are many varieties of Weaving, each with its special appeal. Some Fs, no doubt, prefer the Subtle Weave, which is executed with the delicacy of a gavotte. In this, the tail is held erect, and the human legs are scarcely touched. Others may have a preference for the Hind-Leg Weave, which explains itself with pussy rearing up and rubbing her neck against the legs. For myself, I most enjoy Butting Weave, and I like it to be executed with the greatest energy and enthusiasm. 'Five' is the supreme exponent of this type of weave; he butts his head against my legs as though he were playing football, darts away, turns and butts again; one would think he was trying to knock me down.

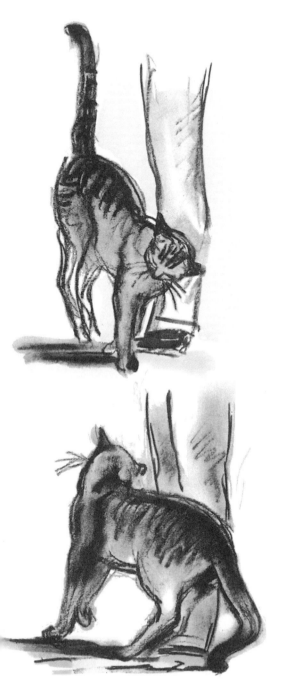

A moment ago I mentioned that one of the stimuli which induce a cat to weave is the aroma of boiling fish. This was perhaps an unwise remark, for it may be cited by the non-F as a proof of his familiar contention that feline affection is only cupboard love. 'A dog loves a man for himself, a cat only loves a man for what he can get out of him.' That is the argument, and a very ignorant and unjust argument it is.

Let us address a few words to the non-F in order that he may be better informed about dogs, cats and their respective capacities for affection. He is grossly misinformed if he assumes that cats love less deeply than dogs. Like a dog, a cat may die of a broken heart. But cats, being cats, are more subtle in the manner in which they manifest their feelings, and more selective in the choice of those persons on whom they bestow their favours. Most Fs will agree that to gain the love of a cat you must have, in yourself, some quality that is lovable.

Supposing that one owns a dog, and that one is returning home after a holiday. The dog will come running out in an ecstasy of joy, barking and leaping and fussing and sniffing, and it is all most endearing and satisfying. We all like to feel that somebody desires us, and to be desired so much, to be missed so passionately, is very flattering to the human ego.

With cats there is no such demonstration. On the contrary. Cats take a very different view of their owners' absences. They seem to feel themselves personally affronted. This is particularly the case with Siamese. Once, after I had been in America for a couple of months, I returned un-expectedly to find Gaskin out. My Siamese cat 'One' was lying on a chair in the hall. As soon as I entered he rose, cast upon me a look of withering scorn, stalked out into the Conserva-tory, sat down on the mat, hoisted his leg, and proceeded to indulge in the intimacies of the toilet. '*That*,' he seemed to be saying, 'will teach you.'

I am not prone to putting words into the mouths of animals and I always feel embarrassed when char-ladies tell stories about their dogs or their cats, beginning with the words 'He looked at me, as much as to say ... ' However, on this occasion 'One' really did look at me 'as much as to say', and I fancy that I know what he was thinking. Something like this:

'So you have come home. And about time too! You need not imagine that you can come strolling back into my life, after weeks of neglect, and expect me to behave as though nothing had happened. Here

have I been, all this time, carrying on the duties of the household, while you have been gadding about, enjoying yourself. I have worked my claws to the bone on your sofa. I have put in a great deal of work on the new curtains and I have demolished quantities of seed beds. I have sat for hours at the drawing-room window, studying the passers-by in the lane, and I have made quantities of notes. And all the time, you have been away. You have left it all to *me*. True, Gaskin has been the soul of courtesy and consideration, but that is not enough. No *sir*! This will all need very serious consideration before I decide upon my future attitude.'

A final touch to the toilet preparations, a last glance of scorn, and out stalks 'One' into the garden in the direction of the orchard into which he disappears with a sharp twitch of his tail. And it is not till nearly three days later, after a great deal of explanation on my part, and many hours of following him round the house, that at last he relents, allowing himself to be stroked, and rewards me with a purr.

Cats, in short, are the only animals who have mastered the art of sending their owners to Coventry — the only animals who know how to put us in our places. But if we behave ourselves, if we are regular in our attendance and if we avoid any of the grosser social errors, they are infinitely rewarding in their kindness.

How many times has my heart been cheered when I walk up the road of a summer evening and see, perched on the wall in the dusk, the familiar figure of 'Five' waiting to greet me. And how many times, when I have stroked him, has he begun to 'weave' with such enthusiasm that he has actually fallen off the wall. How many times, too, have I seen Oscar, sitting on the steps like a carven Sphinx ... a Sphinx that suddenly comes to life and walks slowly towards me with the fading sunlight glinting in his eyes. And how many times, as I have bent down to savour the scent of the tobacco flowers, has a small black shape materialized from the shadows, and the quiet evening has heard the music of 'Four's' purr. These are the moments when we reap the richest rewards that come to the great family of Fs — moments of twilight and quietness, when we seem to speak the same language, and when we meet, as equals, in a world of peace.

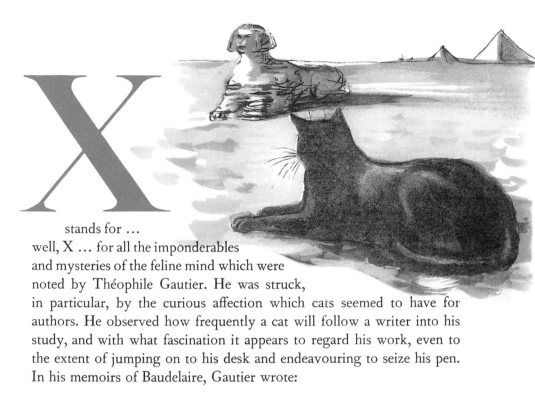

X

stands for ...
well, X ... for all the imponderables
and mysteries of the feline mind which were
noted by Théophile Gautier. He was struck,
in particular, by the curious affection which cats seemed to have for
authors. He observed how frequently a cat will follow a writer into his
study, and with what fascination it appears to regard his work, even to
the extent of jumping on to his desk and endeavouring to seize his pen.
In his memoirs of Baudelaire, Gautier wrote:

> They come to sit on the table by the writer, keeping his thoughts
> company, and gazing at him with intelligent tenderness and magical
> penetration. It seems as though cats divine the thought that is
> passing from the brain to the pen, and that as they stretch out a paw
> they are trying to seize it on its way.

Many non-Fs will tell you that they do not like cats because 'you
never know what they are thinking'. This has always seemed to me a
rather curious stricture, since it would serve with equal force as a reason
for condemning the entire human race. However, non-Fs have never been
noted for their logic.

X would seem a suitable section for a few words about the
Sphinx who, as we have already observed, is so constantly evoked by the
feline poets. When I was at school, I went through the usual period of
decadence and fell for a while under the spell of Oscar Wilde whose poem
'The Sphinx' is literature's nearest approach to a Fabergé cigarette box.
The spell did not last for long, probably because Wilde — though most
people would disagree — was fundamentally non-F. It is not without
interest to recall that one of the grossest examples in history of non-Fness

was offered by the film production of *The Picture of Dorian Gray*. Hollywood, confronted with the task of adapting this curious fable to the taste of the average American schoolgirl, was in something of a quandary. Dr Kinsey had not yet lifted the veil on the private life of American undergraduates, and the Wolfenden Report was still lying, like a small unexploded bomb, in the womb of Time. So what did Hollywood do? The first thing, obviously, was to ensure that the role of Dorian was played by a young gentleman who would have been ideally cast as the captain of a football team. This was successfully arranged, and Dorian's languid epigrams were barked out, with obvious distaste, in tones that recalled the accents of a baseball coach. But this was not enough. Here was a story of evil and since Hollywood could not afford to admit the existence of *that* sort of evil, another victim must be found. So Hollywood chose the cat. In the centre of Dorian's fabulous apartment they placed a large statue of a cat, carved in the Egyptian manner. And whenever Dorian was moved by any of his illicit urges, and stamped his way out of the room, en route to nameless orgies, the cat was spot-lit, and the camera slowly tracked in to a close-up of it ... as though the poor creature was at the root of the trouble. The suggestion, presumably, was that if only Dorian had invested in a nice cocker spaniel, all would have been well. This struck me as not only unbelievably stupid but vilely unjust, and caused me to give vent to a series of loud, sustained and faultlessly feline hisses, which eventually led to my removal from the cinema.

Wilde said that all men kill the thing they love; it would be truer to say that all men kill the thing they cannot understand. For instance, I have known non-Fs who were genuinely disturbed and discomfited by the sight of a cat staring out of a window. There it sits, confronted by apparent nothingness ... a blank wall, a deserted garden, or even a night of utter darkness. But the head darts backwards and forwards, the eyes are always intently focused, the tail lashes to and fro, and the whole body is rigid with interest. 'What is that wretched animal looking at?' asks the non-F uneasily. 'There is nothing to see. It gives me the creeps, going on like that about nothing.'

Which is foolish of the non-F. No living creature 'goes on like that about nothing'. I do not know if cats can really see in the dark; one imagines that some degree of light, however faint, is needed by even the exquisitely sensitive feline eyes. But obviously the cat is seeing *something*, some strange drama is being played out there, on that empty lawn, some mysterious shadow play is passing over that blank wall. Maybe the air is tingling with the echoes of some wild music from over the hills, to which our ears are deaf.

Y stands for Yawning.

Cats and dogs yawn in quite different ways and for quite different reasons. The yawn of a dog is seldom a sign of fatigue nor of ennui; often it denotes intense excitement. A London friend of mine owns a small poodle which is perforce left alone in a flat for most of the day. Whenever I am able, I take it for a walk on Hampstead Heath. As soon as I open the door of the flat I am greeted with leaps of such hysterical delight that it is difficult to put Adolphus — for that is the dog's name — on the lead. This delight continues as we walk down the steps and enter the car. Never were there such extravagant demonstrations, such frenzied lickings, such curlings round on the seat, such leapings up to look through the window.

Then the car starts, and Adolphus sits still, quite rigid, staring at me with his pleasing poodle eyes. We are en route, yes, and that is all to the good, but why do we not go faster? Why must I sit at that silly wheel, staring through the glass, when ... so he seems to imagine ... I have only to open the door again to reveal the delights of the wide spaces of the Heath? Evidently he has not yet grasped the relation between time and distance; he does not realize that it takes a while to travel from point A to point B. So suddenly it comes, a long, dramatic yawn that seems to engulf his whole body. This is the absolute opposite of ennui, it is a trembling *crie de cœur*, an agonized protest at the cruel prolongation of his imprisonment.

No cat would every carry on like that. Cats yawn for the sheer sensuous pleasure of it. And often, as they yawn, they arch their necks and stretch out their paws in front of them, as though to intensify that pleasure.

But Y stands for a great deal more than yawning. It is really a convenient device to introduce the whole fascinating subject of Sleep. (The letter 'S', as we have seen, was reserved for 'Stroking'.)

Even in their natural surroundings of the jungle, felines spend a very large proportion of their lives in sleep. This is a fact that offers a grain of consolation when one remembers how many of them have to live in captivity. Sometimes when I pass great blocks of modern flats I look up and think of all the cats and dogs and birds incarcerated behind those bleak façades. The thought would be almost unbearable if one did not re-member that many of them, perhaps, were asleep. And even this thought would be unbearable if one did not believe that one day, when they died, they would wake to an eternal freedom.

Here is a problem that intrigues me; if you are a true F you have probably pondered it yourself. How is it that a cat who has slept through the winter months, week after week, for at least twenty hours out of the twenty-four, a cat who has partaken lavishly during this period of fish and milk, a cat whose only exercise has been to stretch on the carpet, to vault languidly on to the window sill and survey the rain-swept garden, to chatter its teeth for a few moments at the starlings and then to sink back into repose against the radiator ... how is it that such a creature, whom one would have thought to be flabby and utterly out of condition, can suddenly leap into life at the first sign of spring, shoot like an arrow across the lawn, and stream up the trunk of a tree as though it had spent the entire winter in training for the Olympic Games? (Reading over this question it seems the longest that even I have ever written. It would be agony to parse, and what we should have done without those three dots in the middle, I cannot imagine.)

But we will let the question stand. For it really is of interest. A human being who has slept so long and eaten so lavishly would be flabby and short of wind; his stomach would be distended, his muscles would be atrophied, and he would be hard put to it to climb a flight of stairs, let alone a tree. And yet pussy manages it with superb aplomb. Even 'Four', who as we have already observed is over eighty in human terms still leaps up the weeping-willow with the utmost grace, and perches on the top in the centre, where he looks like a sort of mad, black toque perched on the untidy head of a witch. One shudders to think of one's octogenarian acquaintances indulging in similar activities.

One of the myriad enchantments of living with cats lies in the fact that one never knows with whom one may be passing the night. Is one in favour? Will there be a small black shape ... 'Four' ... curled up on the foot of the bed? Or a plump black and white ball of fur ... 'Five' ... disposed primly in the middle? Or a huge, lean, mottled creature ... Oscar ... guarding the pillow?

Or will there be nobody at all? Will 'Four' have decided that the charms of the radiator exceed those of his master? Will 'Five' have deserted me for Gaskin? And will Oscar merely be absent, intent upon some mysterious errand in the shrubbery?

Sometimes, on gala nights, 'Four' and 'Five' both come to the conclusion that I am in need of noctural consolation. (Not Oscar, who never shares his favours.) Quite frankly, these occasions are not an unmixed delight. Naturally, one cannot dismiss them both; still less can one dismiss only one of them. To do so would be construed as a sign of gross favouritism, and might set up a number of deep-rooted complexes. So one pretends to be enchanted, and slithers through the sheets, forcing a passage for one's body between 'Four', who is probably draped round one's ankles, and 'Five', who reclines like an enormous furry hot-water-bottle in the crook of one's knees. And then one turns out the light and hopes for the best ... hopes that one will not get cramp, that 'Four' will not decide that he would be more comfortable on one's stomach, that 'Five' will not hear the owl hooting outside and jump up and scratch at the door to be let out, and that the soft duet of purrs will slowly lull one to sleep.

An awful thought has suddenly assailed me. I have just remembered the young woman from Bexhill-on-Sea.

She is the very last person whom I should have wished to remember, at a tranquil moment like this, but since she has intruded herself, she must be dealt with ... severely. For all I know, there may be others like her, lurking in sea-side resorts around our coasts.

About a year ago, this young woman who lives at Bexhill-on-Sea wrote me a very rude letter out of the blue. Apparently she has heard that I sometimes have cats sleeping on my bed at night, and the information disgusted her. 'Of all the unhygienic habits!!!' she exclaimed. (She was one of those correspondents whose pen spouts exclamation marks.) 'How *can* you? If I ever had any children I should punish them severely if I ever caught them with cats on their beds!!! What about the *germs?*' To which one might retort that if she felt so strongly about germs in bed she would probably never have any children at all. I would swop the entire microbic content of 'Four' and 'Five' for that of one energetic young sanitary inspector.

This letter from Bexhill-on-Sea not only angered but astonished me, because I happen to be President of the Bexhill-on-Sea Cat Club, which is a highly geared, streamlined organization, with a powerful influence in the concerns of that resort. I have been given to understand that the favour of the Bexhill-on-Sea Cat Club is eagerly sought — as it should be — by persons aspiring to seats on the local council, and that those upon whom it frowns have little chance of achieving eminence. In so civilized a locality one would have thought that there would be no place for young women with such grossly incorrect notions about cats sleeping on beds. Evidently one was wrong, and something must be done. One must Use One's Influence.

And that will be enough for the young lady from Bexhill-on-Sea.

Now for a word about cats' sleeping quarters. In their choice of couches cats show an exquisite ingenuity. They reveal themselves as domestic sybarites, with an uncanny facility for finding the warmest quarters of the house, and as jungle realists, who are never forgetful of the dangers of sudden attack. True, in a normal household this danger is seldom more acute than the sudden onslaught of the daily woman with carpet-sweeper. (I have spoken to Gaskin dozens of times about that daily woman but she still comes. She is enough to drive one mad. She stands in the middle of the music-room in a sort of trance, pushing the carpet-sweeper up and down as though she were fanning herself. When she is not doing this she is drinking such enormous quantities of tea that one's own stomach shudders in sympathy. The cats hate her, and I hate her, and I cannot believe that those rattling carpet-sweepers do any good. But she still comes. However, this is a domestic 'aside' that will probably be struck out in the proofs.[1])

To return to this bed business. Let me tell you about the most beautiful bed in the whole world, which once belonged to 'Five'. This was the linen cupboard at Merry Hall — my old house that has gone with the wind. It was a haven of warmth, and quiet, and peace and utter security. Tell me if you can imagine any sweeter place of repose. You walked up an old Georgian staircase, with the sunlight slanting through the delicate slits of the balustrade. Ahead of you was 'Five', with his bushy tail very erect, for pleasure was in store, and sleep, in such perfect surroundings

---

[1] As you will observe, it was not. The woman has been struck out instead.

as he anticipated, would be not merely a passive abandonment of care, it would be an active pleasure. You passed down a corridor and 'Five's' tail switched to the right, into a shadowy little alcove which concealed the entrance to the linen cupboard. There was a faint mew, a glint of green eyes as 'Five' looked up at you, and the gentle extension of a paw. Then you opened the door, and the haven of the linen cupboard was revealed.

Haven, indeed, it was. Warm, roomy, dark, mysterious — but mysterious in a way that breathed a strange friendliness. Shelf upon shelf of sheets and blankets and pillow-slips, with here and there an eiderdown or a bed cover that had faded, and in the top left-hand corner a patchwork quilt. Everything was well worn and familiar, and some of the sheets would soon be sent to the laundry for the last time. But everything proclaimed peace.

And then, 'Five' would spring up on to the first shelf, pausing for a moment to stick his tail up and indulge in a few delicate kneading movements with his paws. Then over and up to the second shelf, and the third, which was the elevation that most suited him. Whereupon he would turn round and round with great fastidiousness between an old pink blanket and a quilt and a couple of ancient curtains, until finally he had made a 'nest'. (My mother once told me that the reason why cats turned round in circles before lying down to sleep was because they remembered the old days in the jungle, when they had to flatten down the long grasses in order to make a bed. My mother had a large store of these charming little tit-bits of science. I see no reason why they should not be true.)

So now the picture is complete, with 'Five' in his nest, and his green eyes glinting in the semi-darkness, and the gentle warmth of the radiators creeping up to soothe him. And now, too, I remember that this section comes under Y. So we will allow him the luxury of a last Yawn, and close the door — or rather, leave it ajar — and tiptoe away.

Z stands for ...

Whatever else we may decide that Z stands for, it does not stand for Zoos. This is a book in which no institution so miserable as a Zoo should play any part. I am totally unable to understand the general public's attitude to Zoos. There are thousands of normal kindly women with cats and dogs of their own — women who would be outraged if they were accused of cruelty, who nevertheless see nothing in the least objectionable in seizing wild animals, dragging them from their natural environment and incarcerating them for life — for *life*, mind you — in cages so small that they can hardly turn. Not only do these people see nothing wrong in this practice but they take their horrible children to glare at the animals, and giggle and throw buns and poke sticks. And then, having thoroughly warped and perverted their infant minds they express astonishment when their darlings grow up to be 'juvenile delinquents' ... which is the modern euphemism for immature thugs.

I have — and so, I imagine, have you — a number of favourite day-dreams, though day-dreams is not quite the right expression, as I usually indulge them at twilight. There is the day-dream when I am a millionaire, able to employ innumerable slaves in creating the perfect garden, waving a hand and saying: 'Let there be balustrades and terraces

and fountains, and kindly cover the entire slopes of that hill over with daffodils ... *at once*.' (There have been several occasions in the past, when I have forgotten that this was a day-dream, and have begun to put the idea into practice, which is the reason why I shall probably end up in an old gentlemen's home.) There is another day-dream where I have a sort of magic box which emits incredibly powerful and mysterious rays, rather like the instruments of destruction which figure so largely in space fiction. In this dream I float gaily round the world, turning my rays on to persons who seem to be more than usually objectionable at the moment — dictators, child-beaters and sadists in general. During the rape of Hungary my box was in such constant and concentrated use that it is a wonder there were any rays left in it. But there were and ... I warn you ... there still are.

But in my favourite day-dream of all, reserved for very special occasions, when the twilight is lit with a magic glow and the psychic influences are at their most powerful, I have discovered a secret key that unlocks all the cages at the Zoo. And I tiptoe through the entrance, and turn all the locks and fling open all the gates, beginning of course at the smaller cat section. And there is a roaring and a raging and a gnashing of teeth and a flashing of wild, accusing eyes. And the animals rush past me and leap over the railings, and flood the highways and byways of northern London in a vast avenging stream. They crash through the windows of respectable parlours and descend on plump families watching television and send their teeth crunching through the fat bottoms of the ladies who, for so many years, have been insulting them with buns. They pick up overfed little boys with a single, exquisite gesture and hurl them over the roof. They pounce on prosperous city men, rip off their clothes, and propel them like pingpong balls into the icy waters of the Regent's Canal. And then licking their lips, purring ferociously — but far from satisfied — they depart *en masse*, to deal with the directors.

You must admit that this is a most pleasing day-dream, and I should feel comforted if I thought that you might sometimes indulge it. If enough people dream the same dream, there is always the chance that one day it might come true.

★   ★   ★

This is perhaps a jarring note on which to end my little book, which has been written mainly in accordance with the legend engraved on ancient sundials ... 'I count only the sunlit hours.' But all Fs will agree with me that if one loves animals one has to pay for it, and that the pains and sorrows of the animal world can wring our hearts as acutely as any of the woes of mankind. Sometimes, when I have come across some animal in distress and when — as so often — I have been tragically incompetent to do anything about it, I have wished that there were some sort of pill which one could swallow, to numb the heart and steel the brain against pity. Anti-Pity Pills would make life simpler in a hundred ways, and I greatly envy the number of persons who appear to have access to an unlimited supply of them.

Failing such a potion, the best one can do, in order that life should not be one long heart-ache, is to try to be intelligent. Above all, to avoid the emotional snares of excessive anthropomorphism. To credit an animal with the same pains and fears as one feels in one's own body is, I think, unjustified. (At least, I very much hope so!) Obviously, there are degrees of pain, and it is not unreasonable to suppose that they vary in intensity according to the sensitivity of the sufferer. A migraine in the brain of a Shelley or Mozart, one imagines, would be more agonizing than in the brain of an all-in-wrestler. Going down the scale, the wrestler might suffer more acutely than the Australian aboriginal, who in his turn might suffer more than the chimpanzee, who has a more delicate nervous system than the bulldog and so on almost *ad infinitum*, until we come down to the lowest form of animal life, the sea anemone on the rocks. This, at least, is how I try to comfort myself when I see a lost kitten. I tell myself that it is not really so bad as if it were a lost baby.

And yet, even with sea anemones, it distresses me when small boys poke their fingers into them and bruise them, and make them close their delicate, waving limbs. After all, sea anemones *are* a form of life and a very beautiful form of life; they must experience some form of joy and delight on their secret rocks, with the green waters drifting over them, and the sunlight filtering through. Equally they must experience some form of terror and dismay when they are brutally assaulted.

I am well aware that these are unfashionable sentiments which, to many, will appear absurd. I have served, too often, as a target for ridicule to be unaware of the rich gift which I am handing to the satirist. 'Humanity in peril of extinction ... and Nichols drools about sea anemones!' That is one obvious line of attack. It does not greatly concern me. There is a reverse side to every argument, and it might not be unreasonable to suggest that if more people began to concern themselves with such humble creatures as sea anemones they might, as they ascended the ladder of life, show more consideration for humanity. In any case, it is not so very intelligent to despise the sea anemones; they were our original ancestors and after we have reaped the whirlwind they may, once again, be the only form of life that stirs in the waters of an empty world.

Which reminds me that it is time to give the cats their fish. For the past twenty minutes there have been restless movements in the corridor, the sound of impatient scratchings on the carpet, and even heads protruding round the edge of my study door. So I will lay down my pen and attend to more important business. You remember the routine? 'Four' under the kitchen sink, 'Five' on the table, and Oscar by the side of the dresser. When I think of such pleasant little domestic conventions I feel that life, after all, has a pattern, and makes some sort of sense.